CONTENTS

Reste: <u>1$</u> x Lapin ± salsify
_____
0 x Pigeon → Lapin cote

L x Epaule

8 x Jalapenos 2

PARIS

A pocket guide to the city's best
cultural hangouts, shops, bars
and eateries

DONNA WHEELER

Hardie Grant
TRAVEL

INTRODUCTION

Beloved for its elegance and grandeur, cultural riches and romantic streetscapes, Paris is also a city that's dedicated to pleasure and beauty. Life here contains many fascinating contradictions. Despite the presence of history at every turn, it's an undeniably modern, progressive city, one that in the last ten years has cast off its 'museum-ified' reputation and welcomed a new wave of restaurateurs, retailers, hoteliers and entrepreneurs. It's a city where you can party till dawn, or spend your days quietly communing with its cultural treasures. It's a city that dictates global fashions and trends but also doggedly holds dear to long-established daily routines.

Paris began as a walled settlement on the river Seine's Île de la Cité, with marshlands to the north and fields and vineyards to the south. The still remarkably compact centre is home to 2.2 million of greater Paris' 12 million inhabitants – and easy to navigate by foot, bike or Metro. It's been divided into administrative areas called arrondissements since the French Revolution, spiralling out in a clockwise direction from the centre's 'Premier' or 1st. Since 1860, when Baron Haussmann razed and rebuilt much of the city's ancient heart, creating the graceful boulevards that are Paris' calling card today, these have numbered up to twenty.

The city's great geographical divider is the Seine, giving the city its 'rive gauche' and 'rive droit' – the Left and Right Banks, the Left once tending to bohemian and intellectual, the Right once the centre of power and commerce. Current chroniclers of the city point out that a more obvious social division today runs east to west. The east being the playground of the young and fashionable, home to immigrant communities, globally relevant and occasionally still revolutionary; the west being where the civic institutions, the wealthy and historical monuments are found.

Even on repeat visits, Paris' sheer beauty can make it feel like a waking dream, but it is, at the same time, a deeply complex, layered and defiantly real place. Let me guide you to monuments, little-known museums, shops, local cafes and bars with *Paris Pocket Precincts*, your curated guide to the world's most visited city.

Donna Wheeler

A PERFECT PARIƧ DAY

As the saying goes, Paris is always a good idea, even when most Parisians are asleep. The city isn't known for its early risers and grabbing a coffee first thing can prove tricky. So after I drag myself out of bed, I'll go for a quick poke around the **Marché d'Aligre**, or perhaps a quiet stroll up through **Cimetière du Père Lachaise**. After, I'll head to **Shakespeare and Company Café** for a café noisette when they open at 9.30am. Then to **Musée Rodin** to visit my favourite sculptures and drawings before some contemplation in the gardens. If it's a day for indulging, I'll settle in for a four-course Basque blowout at **l'Ami Jean**, though in summer, I'll cross the Seine and it'll be leeks vinaigrette or carpaccio at **Maison Maison** by the river-facing windows. A post-prandial micro-nap might be needed at this point, so I'll find a chair at the **Jardin du Palais-Royal**. I'll then have a window shop beneath its colonnades, swing past **Brigitte Tanaka** and along the Faubourg Saint-Honoré. Or if I need to pick up a shirt or tee, I'll head to the Marais' rue des Francs Bourgeois. I'll peek at the newest installation at the nearby **Musée de la Chasse et de la Nature**, then grab a sweet treat at **Chambelland** up in the 11th. On the way out again in the evening, I'll swing past **Le Baron Rouge** for a sneaky Muscadet, then **Vélib** (bike share) up to Canal Saint-Martin and try for a table at neobistro **Le Verre Volé** or otherwise head to **Déviant** for standing room small plates, a Tunisian brik and natural wine. I'll head back to the Seine, lingering along the **Bassin de l'Arsenal** before heading home, but if kicking-on is on the cards, I'll meet friends for bar-hopping along the rue du Faubourg Saint-Denis, with cocktails at **Le Syndicat**, before a midnight DJ set at **La Java**. If I'm in for a really big night or there's a band I know playing, I'll head to Pigalle, where things will quite possibly go on till dawn (did I mention Parisians aren't early risers?).

PARIS OVERVIEW

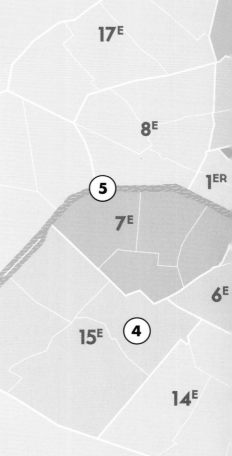

PRECINCTS

FIELD TRIPS

PARIS

18ᴱ

⑨

19ᴱ

⑬

9ᴱ

⑥

10ᴱ

⑦

2ᴱ

②

3ᴱ

①

③

20ᴱ

⑩

11ᴱ

4ᴱ

④

8ᴱ

5ᴱ

12ᴱ

④

13ᴱ

⑫ 🚆

LE PREMIER, 1ST

'Le Premier' arrondissement is Paris' literal and historical heart. Over a quarter of it is taken up by the Jardin des Tuileries, so at some point you'll undoubtedly find yourself in this one-time garden of Catherine de Medici, a beloved public park since the French Revolution. Meander around its ponds, down broad avenues, past (overpriced) cafes and among the hubbub of its summertime funfair. To one side, you'll find the equally historic and expansive Louvre museum (*see* p. 2), as well as the rue di Rivoli, the retail golden mile of rue Saint-Honoré and the stately Palais-Royal (*see* p. 4). Along with the 8th arrondissement, this is also where most of the city's famed five-star hotels, such as Le Meurice, the Ritz and newcomer Nolinksi, cluster.

Les Halles was, until the 1970s, the city's legendary food market and its surrounding streets are still fun to explore with round-the-clock diners and restaurant supply shops that once serviced the market traders and customers. The 1st also takes in a small slice of the Seine's largest island, the Île de la Cité and the glorious stone Pont Neuf, spanning the Seine, with its dual arches and bronze and equine statue of King Henri IV.

Metro: Louvre Rivoli, Pyramides, Pont Neuf, Palais-Royal Musée du Louvre, Châtelet

→ *View to Pont Neuf from the Quai du Louvre*

1 MUSÉE DU LOUVRE

rue de Rivoli, 75001
01 40 20 53 17
www.louvre.fr/en
Open Wed–Mon 9am–6pm,
Wed & Fri until 9.45pm
Metro Palais-Royal Musée
du Louvre
[MAP p. 183 A1]

You can't avoid the crowds
(8 million visitors a year!), and
a sense of overwhelm is almost
inevitable (35,000 works of
art on show!), but what you
get is one of the world's most
extraordinary collections of
western art, and a wander
through one of Louis XIV's
most stunning 16th-century
palaces. You'll probably visit
the *Mona Lisa* (Room 6,
1st floor, Denon wing), the
Venus de Milo (Room 16,
ground floor, Sully wing) and
perhaps a Raphael, Titian or
Botticelli. But the real don't-
miss is *Liberty Leading the
People*, Eugene Delacroix's
revolutionary masterwork
(aka *Les Trois Glorieuses*, in
room 75, Denon wing), where
you might also notice Théodore
Géricault's great, stonking
Raft of the Medusa. Egyptian,
Mesopotamian and Byzantine
antiquities (in the Richelieu,
Sully and Denon wings,
respectively) will enchant
too. For a more contained
experience, plan your visit to
see key collections or come at
night for an exhibition.

POCKET TIP
For a delightful counter to
the crowds and high culture,
the Musée des Arts Décoratifs
(MAD) is in the Louvre's
western wing, Pavillon
de Marsan; their fashion
exhibitions are particularly
mind-blowing.

2 JEU DE PAUME

1 Place de la Concorde, 75001
01 47 03 12 50
www.jeudepaume.org
Open Tues 11am–9pm,
Wed–Sun 11am–7pm
Metro Concorde, Tuileries
[MAP p. 176 A3]

POCKET TIP

The lobby shop has an excellent book selection and good kitsch-free gifts, and there's a light and calm cafe with a broad shady summer terrace.

This dedicated national museum is the city's most consistently compelling place to catch international contemporary shows of photography, video art and new technology with an international outlook. Past exhibitions have showcased the works of the likes of Cindy Sherman, Martin Parr, William Kentridge, Ed Ruscha and Gordon Matta-Clark. Concurrent shows of mid-careerists and boundary pushers from France or the Francophone world are also good. The building, originally royal tennis courts during the Second Empire, also has a fascinating, if tragic, World War II history. During the occupation of Paris, it was used by the Nazis as a sorting house for stolen Jewish collections, with over 22,000 individual works. Curator Rose Valland's tireless record keeping at the time, Resistance ties and post-war persistence ensured at least some works were finally returned to their rightful owners.

3 PALAIS-ROYAL

8 rue de Montpensier, 75001
Open daily 7am–11pm
Metro Palais-Royal Musée
du Louvre
[MAP p. 177 D4]

Pull up an iron chair and join Parisian freelancers, dreamers and shoppers circling the formal garden's fountain for sun worship and a snatch of shut eye. Once a regal palace and 17th-century 'town in the city' prototype, the Palais-Royal transformed in the 1830s to the complex of formal gardens, shops, cafes and shaded 'galleries' that exist today. A one-time hotbed of intellectual ferment and carnal abandon, its calm internal arcades today cloister many of the city's most fashionable shops (such as **Rick Owens**), some excellent upmarket restaurants and coffee-stop **Café Kitsune**. The dreamy treescapes, rose beds and high fashion window displays might be Palais-Royal's most obvious drawcards, but Daniel Buren's **Les Deux Plateaux** installation – aka Colonnes de Buren – must be its most photographed. Black and white candy-striped marble columns – all 260 of them – were a controversial conceptual commission in 1986 but today are an absolute must-do for kissing couples, skateboarders and selfie-takers.

POCKET TIP

The Musée de l'Orangerie
(Jardin des Tuileries) is
home to eight sublimely
immersive Water Lilies
murals by Claude Monet,
along with Cézannes
and Modiglianis.

5

4 A/TIER DE VILLATTE

173 rue Saint Honoré, 75001
01 42 60 74 13
www.astierdevillatte.com
Open Mon–Sat 11am–7pm
Metro Tuileries, Palais-Royal
Musée du Louvre
[MAP p. 176 C4]

Ivan Pericoli and Benoît Astier de Villatte's aesthetic is not limited to their milky-glazed black ceramic tableware but also adds a wistful, theatrical edge to everything from candles and colognes to paper weights, badges, scented erasers and notebooks. The shop was once a silversmith frequented by Napoleon; now window displays of surreal whimsy often highlight a recent collaboration, while within little seems to have changed. The creaking wooden shelves, layers of paint and faded wallpaper make the ethereal ceramics (all handmade and following traditional techniques), seem all the more precious and mysterious. If you're not in the market for one of these unique treasures, a Commune de Paris candle in tri-colour ceramic (a collaboration with the Parisian menswear brand) is scented with a 19th-century blend of Sicilian lemon, geranium and coumarin, or you can take your pick of many others.

5 BRIGITTE TANAKA

18 rue Saint-Roch, 75001
01 42 96 30 49
www.brigittetanaka.com
Open Mon–Sat 11am–2pm &
3–7pm
Metro Pyramides
[MAP p. 176 C4]

This tiny three-storey shopfront must be the world's most petite concept store. Owners Brigitte Giraudi and Chieko Tanaka's vision is a beautiful hybrid of the pretty and the utilitarian, the Japanese and the French, the vintage and the freshly handcrafted, the elegant and the quirky. Limited edition collaborations include delicate jewellery (budget-friendly as it's all costume), linens, leather accessories, stationery and useful seasonal things, such as pure sheepskin shoe inserts for keeping the cold at bay or rattan market bags for summer picnicking. Souvenir hunters can go for the subtle red, white and blue Moroccan slippers or a hilariously literal baguette lamp, that glows as if it's still in the oven. Head down the spiralling stone stairs – a relic of the shop's previous life as a seller of religious trinkets for the neighbouring Eglise Saint-Roch – to have your ceramics kiln-branded with your initial in 18-carat gold, or venture up to have them embroidered on napkins or bathrobes.

POCKET TIP
For fuss-free lingerie and swimsuits with a '70s rock and roll vibe, head to Yasmine Eslami (35 rue de Richelieu).

6 E. DEHILLERIN

18–20 rue Coquillière, 75001
01 42 36 53 13
www.edehillerin.fr/en
Open Mon 9am–12.30pm &
2–6pm, Tues–Sat 9am–6pm
Metro Louvre Rivoli, Les Halles
[MAP p. 177 E4]

Cooks of all persuasions, from professionals to happy amateurs, will get that little thrill that only seeing so much cookware in one spot can bring. Copper pots, pans and dishes can be found in the basement for those looking for lifetime companions, but the baking equipment right near the entrance includes an incredible range of packable financier tins, pastry molds, piping nozzles and balloon whisks. Until 1971, Les Halles was Paris' main produce market, and this packed-to-the-rafters cookware shop, and others like it in the precinct, is a legacy of when chefs would shop for their daily ingredients at the market and then swing by here to pick up a new pot or rolling pin. Don't expect bargains, but you'll definitely find things here you won't find anywhere else (and things you never knew you needed until now), like a Breton crêpe pan for turning out authentic galettes (savoury buckwheat pancakes).

POCKET TIP
The drab '80s shopping mall Forum des Halles that replaced Les Halles has had a 21st-century makeover; it's beloved by Parisian teenagers, but it's still a mall.

7 LA PÂTISSERIE DU MEURICE PAR CÉDRIC GROLET

6 rue de Castiglione, 75001
01 44 58 10 10
www.dorchestercollection.com
Open Tues–Sun 12pm–6pm
Metro Tuileries
[MAP p. 177 B3]

So you've had a macaron or two in your time, know your way around a Paris-Brest and are oh so familiar with frangipane fillings? Then Cédric Grolet is your pâtissier. The official pastry chef for 5-star hotel Le Meurice, and voted the best in the world in 2017, Grolet's creations were once only available for hotel guests and those taking tea. Now his brass and stone workshop just around the corner welcomes all, and staff toil over tarts, glaze fruit and pipe crème-pâtissière in front of your eyes. Grolet's style rests firmly in French tradition but he uses far less sugar and he's fond of riffing on the natural flavours of a key ingredient. His famous trompe-l'œil apples, a kouglof or tart to share, come glamourously packaged and are surprisingly affordable. In-shop photo ops are encouraged – it's all a joyful celebration of the seasons and the pâtissier's art. Note: the shop closes once the day's wares are sold; if you're after a large tart, order 48 hours in advance.

POCKET TIP

For gluten-free, try these cafes: Helmut Newcake (9th); Noglu Restaurant & Épicerie (2nd); Wild and the Moon (various locations).

8 TÉLE/COPE

5 rue Villedo, 75001
01 42 61 33 14
Open Mon–Fri 8.30am–5pm,
Sat 9.30am–6.30pm
Metro Pyramides
[MAP p. 177 D3]

One of the vanguard figures in Paris' coffee revolution, Nicolas Clerc is still turning out perfect café noisettes and café crèmes from locally roasted beans on his Marzocco espresso machine daily at Télescope, a firm favourite with the city's coffee cognoscenti. Nic and his band of bilingual regulars are always up for a chat; 'I baked the financiers myself … do you think they're moist enough?' he may enquire when you come to pay your bill. Delightfully unassuming and friendly, Télescope does, however, have notable exactitudes – the carefully sourced soughdough bread used in its sandwiches, good croissants; and the deliciously perverse step to declare itself a wi-fi and laptop-free zone in an increasingly wired city. If the tables and stools are all taken, grab yours to go, and head to that sublimely pretty, rose-filled Jardin du Palais-Royal (*see* p. 4).

POCKET TIP
For specialist roasters and 'third wave' cafes head to Honor (1st); Matamata (2nd) and Lomi (18th).

11

9 MAISON MAISON

16 Quai du Louvre, 75001
09 67 82 07 32
www.restaurant-maisonmaison.com
Open Tues–Sat 10am–11pm
Metro Louvre Rivoli
[MAP p. 183 B2]

That such a rustic cabanon – that's French for 'shack' – exists in the 1st arrondissement seems unlikely enough. That the said shack comes with uninterrupted views of the Seine (Pont Neuf to your left, Eiffel Tower to your right), fresh sprigs of flowers on the table *and* offers a neat daily roll call of produce-driven, innovative and reasonably priced dishes really is something of a miracle. Lunch menus might include mackerel with cockles and radicchio, a carpaccio of Paris-grown mushrooms with dried, smoked ricotta or duck with olives and red onions. Wine is natural, and there's craft IPAs or artisan pastis. The terrace below, right on the newly pedestrianised Parc Rives de Seine, is splendidly sun-drenched, but during the day is only for drinks or coffee and cake. In the evening, the kitchen switches gear both upstairs and down, sending out a short edit of apéro-hour delights: bulots (sea snails) and mayo, burrata or house-made terrine. Note that breakfast is from 10am to 12pm and it's snacks only from 3pm to 7pm.

10 CHEZ LA VIELLE

1 rue Bailleul, 75001
01 42 60 15 78
www.chezlavieille.fr
Open Tues–Sat 12pm–2pm,
6–10.30pm
Metro Louvre-Rivoli
[MAP p. 183 B1]

An American in Paris, chef Daniel Rose has breathed new life into an historic bistrot while keeping both the cosy proportions and rickety staircase of its 16th-century townhouse. Upstairs there's a hushed, intimate and rather dreamy single room with deep blue walls, ruby banquettes and a large street-facing window. Downstairs a workaday zinc bar is roomier, if for standing only. The menu though is identical both up and down, at lunch and dinner. The signature starter is the bouillon, with spaetzle (noodles), crispy lardons and a soup-coddled egg, though sardine rilletes with seaweed butter and puy lentils with foiegras are also fixtures. Mains blanquette (veal in a white sauce) or boudin Basque aux pommes (Basque black pudding and apple) might sound like French nursery stodge but Rose's defiantly traditional kitchen is also one of flair and precision. A knowing mix of natural and conventional wines, mostly from organic small producers, accompany the soul-bolstering food.

11 I*ADORA

60 rue Jean-Jacques Rousseau,
75001
09 53 13 67 70
www.isadora.paris
Open Tues–Sat 6pm–2am
Metro Palais-Royal Musée du
Louvre, Etienne Marcel
[MAP p. 177 E4]

Paris is suddenly full of
'secret' bars in basements and
self-proclaimed speakeasies,
though social media
coverage make many seem
like just another tourist-clad
(overpriced) drinking hole.
Where to go when you want
a deliciously louche interior,
a touch of exclusive frisson
and a credible DJ soundtrack?
Isadora invites high-heels
and eyeliner, but T-shirts will
work as well, and there's no
queues and no attitude. The
little shopfront's 19th-century
murals of deep green exotic
forests conjure places distant
in time and space; and the
cocktails, spirits and sparklings
on offer are all French and
all top shelf. There's also the
occasional surprise, from rock
star live sets, performance art
pop-ups, a burlesque and the
odd famous indie actor doing
shots at the bar. During Paris
Fashion Week in October and
February, and the FIAC and
ParisPhoto art fairs, call ahead
to make sure it's not closed for
private functions.

SENTIER, MONTORGUEIL & BOURSE, 2ND

Paris' smallest arrondissement was once the preserve of bankers and business suits, but while it's still home to the Bourse, the city's stock exchange, it's also where you can find fabulously vibrant, low-key corners to kick back in. The fashion district of Étienne Marcel, which takes in rue Montmartre, rue du Jour and rue Tiquetonne, is flush with the shops of young designers, streetwear labels and vintage dealers. This happy fashion zone segues nicely into the pedestrianised rue Montorgueil, a convivial strip for eating, drinking and produce shopping. At rue Montorgueil's northern end, the rag trade roots of Sentier are still in evidence, with wholesale outlet and workshop strips, but the precinct has also become something of a start-up hub, with a growing number of bars, cafes and restaurants, along with boutique hotels catering to a young tech crowd and other assorted global creatives. You'll find some of the last remaining shopping arcades (see p. 18) and the grand beacon of Paris' most legendary cinema, Le Grand Rex, shines out from here too.

Metro: Bourse, Bonne-Nouvelle, Sentier, Réaumur-Sébastopol

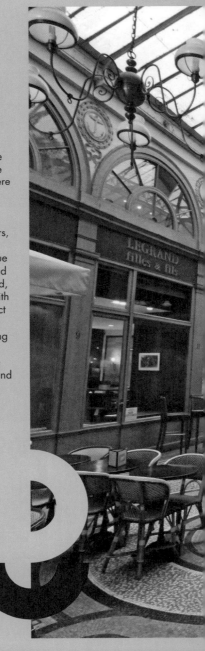

⤙ Galerie Vivienne, an 1823 passage couvert (arcade)

SIGHTS
1. The Arcades

SHOPPING
2. Mad et Len
3. Espace Kiliwatch
4. Sézane

EATING
5. Frenchie Bar à Vins
6. Racines

DRINKING
7. Le Fou
8. Truskel

1 THE ARCADE*

**Metro Grands Boulevards,
Bourse, Sentier**

Paris' passages couverts
(arcades) sprung up across the
city in the early 19th century,
a prototype of the modern
shopping mall and a symbol of
both industrialisation and the
rise of a new class of cashed-up
consumers – the bourgeoise.
Once there were over 150 of
these iron- and glass-roofed
arcades across the city, but
only a handful have survived.
Modern day flâneurs will find
the greatest concentration, and
some of the best preserved,
within a few blocks in the
2nd. Built in 1800, **Passage
des Panoramas** (accessed
from boulevard Montmartre),
has kept its vintage signage,
even if many of its philatelists
and antique dealers have
been replaced by restaurants.
Passage Choiseul (off rue
des Petits Champs), is well
preserved and known for its
dusty second-hand bookshops.
Off rue d'Alexandrie, **Passage
du Caire's** small garment
workshops feel very much like
a Paris of times gone by, while
Galerie Vivienne (off rue
de la Banque), is possibly the
prettiest of them all with its
original intricate mosaics and
designer boutiques.

2 MAD ET LEN

27 Galerie Vivienne, 75002
01 81 70 97 24
Open Tues—Sat 11.30am—
6.30pm
Metro Bourse
[MAP p. 177 D3]

This beautiful space in the heart of the historic **Galerie Vivienne** (see p. 18) has all original fittings and is inspired by traditional apothecary shops. Mad et Len's candles go beyond mere fragrance to create an olfactory journey, one of history, narrative and visceral effect. The creators, who are based in the Verdon Gorges, not far from France's perfume capital Grasse, like to keep things low-key (they don't even have a website), although attention to detail is high. They source all their own essential oils and their candles' notes of wood, fruit, herbs, spices and resins still feel potent and alive. Handpoured and using vegetable soy wax, they are clad in seemingly pre-industrial hand-wrought black iron canisters, sculptural and darkly gothic. Small candles and lava rock 'potpourri' make easily packable gifts and there's a limited range of perfumes too, including 'Paname' – a local nickname for Paris itself – a surprisingly unisex mix of flâneur-friendly tobacco and wild grass.

POCKET TIP
Pick up a bottle of Chablis or Gamay and all the wine wisdom you'll ever need at Legrand Filles et Fils in the Galerie Vivienne.

SENTIER, MONTORGUEIL &
BOURSE, 2ND

3 ESPACE KILIWATCH

64 rue Tiquetonne, 75002
01 42 21 17 37
www.espacekiliwatch.fr
Open Mon–Sat 10.30am–
7.30pm
Metro Étienne Marcel, Sentier
[MAP p. 177 F4]

'Vintage shopping' in Paris can often mean a visit to by-appointment-only dealers who trade in couture or designer pieces that sell for far more than their contemporary counterparts. If you're looking for down-to-earth prices, Kiliwatch offers the more usual endless racks of pre-loved pieces. While you're not necessarily going to uncover any charity shop bargains here, you will find a helpfully themed, range of fripes (old clothes), all in great condition, to pour over, including a whole section dedicated to striped Breton tees. New stock includes jeans, limited-edition sneakers, sunglasses, accessories and seasonal ranges, like French espadrilles in summer or toasty locally sourced knits in winter. Plus there's a nicely curated selection of fashion press in the magazine carrousels. Alexandre Voisin and staff are a hoot and happy to help; if you're a jeans addict, say hi to the bearded Jacques Grosz, who is bonafide Insta-famous and one of Paris' leading denim experts.

POCKET TIP
The last millinery atelier in central Paris, Anthony Peto (56 rue Tiquetonne) turns out traditional styles with a twist at reasonable prices.

POCKET TIP

Demain (3 rue Saint-Fiacre) is Sézane's charity shop, selling clothes from previous seasons and samples, open 21st to 31st of each month.

4 SÉZANE

1 rue Saint Fiacre, 75002
www.sezane.com
Open Tues–Sat 11am–8pm
Metro Grands Boulevards,
Bonne Nouvelle
[MAP p. 177 E2]

Whether you're already hooked on the jeans, jumpers and French-girl florals of this affordable, casual online brand or not, Morgane Sézalory's bricks and mortar flagship – known as l'apartement, and yes it does feel like a light, feminine Parisian home – is a delight. Here you can see, and try on, all the looks you've wish-listed, or, if it's your first encounter, be totally seduced into the Sézane lifestyle. And lifestyle it is, with head-to-toe women's fashion – shoes, bags, scarves and jewellery, plus a growing collection of homewares, not available online. It also stocks books, stationery and other suitcase friendly gifts. If you're handbag shopping, complimentary hot-stamping of your initials is done daily after noon, and if you're keen for any particular style (runs are often limited), order online up to two weeks before you're due in Paris, then pick up at the next door 'concierge'.

5 FRENCHIE BAR À VINS

6 rue du Nil, 75002
01 40 39 96 19
www.frenchie-restaurant.com
Open daily 7–11pm
Metro Sentier, Réaumur-
Sébastopol
[MAP p. 177 F3]

Gregory Marchand's bar sits right across from the original Frenchie restaurant (one of Paris' finest neo-bistros, but also budget-busting). While you'll struggle to book a table there, here at the bar the high stools and communal benches are doled out first come, first served; arrive half an hour before opening and you'll be guaranteed a spot. The sublimely inventive small plates occasionally sync with the restaurant too, and as the bar's menu poetically proclaims they are: 'everything I want to eat, everything'. Ingredients and techniques may often be international – a bao bun here, a scotch egg there, and there's always at least one (very good) pasta dish – but the execution is decidedly French, intriguingly thoughtful. Razor clams come strewn with savoury strawberries and tarragon, melty trout is paired with simple green beans and mint, and Challans duck with plums. A compelling, all small producer wine list and dishy staff (hello, open kitchen!) make for a memorable evening.

POCKET TIP

Francophone cinemaphiles can catch up with latest releases at Le Grand Rex; there's also regular tours of its indeed grand 1930s' interior.

6 RACINE*

8 Passage des Panoramas,
75002
01 40 13 06 41
www.racinesparis.com
Open Mon–Fri 12pm–2pm &
7.30–10pm
Metro Grands Boulevards
[MAP p. 177 E2]

Parisians are all but claiming
burrata, carpaccio and charry-
based margherita pizzas as
their very own at the moment
but you're probably more in
the mood for, well, French
food in Paris. Here's one
Italian, though, you might
want to make a concession
for. Racines occupies a
thoroughly untampered-with
classic bistrots a vins (wine
bistro) space, tucked away
in the historic **Passage des
Panoramas** (*see* p. 18),
which feels as Parisian as
can possibly be. The kitchen
sends out dishes that are far
more interesting and regionally
authentic than the usual Italian
clichés. It's not fancy or slick:
think more an earthy gnocchi
with sausage ragú, polpette
(meatballs), cotoletta (Milanese
schnitzel), braised lamb or
roast chicken. Desserts don't
stray too far from tiramisu or
a hunk of Sardinian cheese,
but they're spot on. Wines
too are mostly Italian, and all
are natural. It's crowded, but
service is attentive and kind
and it's somehow all terribly
romantic, even if you're solo.

POCKET TIP

Rue Sainte-Anne is Paris'
hugely popular Little Tokyo,
with cheap ramen take-
aways, exclusive sushi
restaurants, Japanese grocers
and patisseries trading in
matcha eclairs.

7 LE FOU

37 bis rue du Sentier, 75002
01 40 26 14 94
www.lefou.paris
Open Tues–Fri 7pm–2am,
Sat from 8pm–late
Metro Bonne-Nouvelle, Grands
Boulevards
[MAP p. 177 F2]

Le Fou provides an old-school American bar alternative to Sentier's hotel bars, with huge marble counters, leather seating and dark wood-panelling. There's also a party hard spirit at work with jazz, psych-rock or art school punk down in the basement on the weekends, and a cocktail list that does beautiful renders of the classics but also some Latin specialisms, like Pisco, tequila, lime and bitter chocolate. While there's definitely an old world elegance to it all (the English owner is a great fan of fin-de-siècle Viennese architect Alfred Loos), it somehow seems to conjure high spirits and good vibes rather than the date night hush a cocktail list can sometimes induce. Oh, and there's food – you *may* need some bolstering before heading downstairs – running from porky rillons de Tours and currywurst to truffled gouda and sautéed potatoes.

POCKET TIP

Sentier's most stylish late-night drinking often goes on in the bars of the Hoxton Hotel (with three to choose from), Hotel Edgar or Hotel Bachaumont.

8 TRUSKEL

12 rue Feydeau, 75002
01 40 26 59 97
Open Tues–Sat 6.40pm–5am
Metro Bourse, Grands
Boulevards
[MAP p. 177 E2]

Don't be alarmed – this is not
a Celtic-theme pub. Well, it
does look like one, and there
are big-screen sports and
pints on tap. But as the night
progresses, it moonlights as
a 'micro-club' and live venue,
with nightly DJs playing indie,
Britpop, punk and electro, as
well as a rota of events such
as album launches, mini-
festivals and after-parties.
Pete Doherty, Gruff Rhys, Jarvis
Cocker (the list goes on, but
you get the picture) have all
performed here and although
it is something of a temple to
all things England, live acts
are more commonly of the
very loud and very French
variety. Open late, the drinks
are cheap for this part of town,
it's free to get in and the crowd
is dependably friendly. Also
a good fallback if you fail to
get into David Lynch's nearby
club, Silencio.

THE MARAIS & THE ISLANDS, 3RD & 4TH

Built on what was once marsh land (Marais actually means swamp), much of these two historic arrondissements escaped Baron Haussmann's 19th-century razing, leaving gorgeous 15th- and 16th-century architecture to appreciate today. Down by the Seine, the dense, pretty basse (lower) Marais, the 4th arrondissement, has much of its medieval layout still intact. Pletzl there has long been home to Paris' Jewish population (its rue des Rosiers lined with falafel joints and kosher cake shops), and has also been a hub of Parisian LGBTIQ life since the '70s. The haut (upper) Marais, the 3rd arrondissement, has its own particular charm, with streets of pale 17th-century hôtel particuliers (mansions), tiny courtyard parks and a genteel village feel. The grand Place du Vosges is the oldest square in Paris, bordered on all sides by stunning vaulted walkways and achingly elegant buildings.

If you're in Paris to shop, you'll find one of the city's densest shopping zones where these two arrondissements meet. Every French mid-range label – Bensimon, A.P.C., Isabel Marant, American Vintage, Princesse TamTam, Petit Bateau etc. – has at least one shop in either rue des Francs-Bourgeois, rue Vieille-du-Temple, as well as more again along the sweep of boulevard Beaumarchais and its northern continuation, boulevard Filles-du-Calvaire. Across the Pont Marie and the Pont Notre-Dame lay the fabulously photogenic if increasingly overtouristed Seine islands, Île de la Cité and Île Saint-Louis and that most famous landmark of them all, Cathédrale Notre-Dame de Paris.

Metro: Saint-Paul, Chemin-Vert, Filles du-Calvaire, Rambuteau, Arts et Métiers

→ View across the Marais rooftops to Centre Georges Pompidou

SIGHTS
1. Centre Georges Pompidou
2. Musée de la Chasse et de la Nature

SHOPPING
3. Bensimon Home Autour du Monde
4. Merci
5. Olivia Clergue
6. 0Fr

SHOPPING & EATING
7. Marché des Enfants Rouges

EATING
8. Carbón Paris
9. Grand Café Tortoni

EATING & DRINKING
10. Vin des Pyrénées & Le 1905

DRINKING
11. Au Petit Fer à Cheval

1 CENTRE GEORGE*
POMPIDOU

Place Georges Pompidou,
75004
01 44 78 12 33
www.centrepompidou.fr
Open Wed–Mon 11am–9pm
Metro Rambuteau, Hôtel de Ville
[MAP p. 180 B2]

Controversial as it was 40 years ago, the Pompidou's city block's worth of radical late-20th-century architecture is today one of Paris' most beloved landmarks, as well as one of its most patronised art museums. Then unknown architects Renzo Piano, Jean Prouve and Richard Rogers totally deconstructed the idea of a museum space, what Piano has called 'a brave but impolite' inside-out design, with tube-enclosed escalators and a skin of exposed pipes. The Beaubourg (as it's known to locals) has one of the world's most gobsmacking collections of Modernist and contemporary art, with everyone from Braque, Picasso and Duchamp to Louise Bourgeois, Joseph Beuys and Bill Viola represented. Temporary shows, often held on the top floor, benefit from a thing rare in an art world of white cubes: light and views. The panorama alone is worth a trip up the tube escalators, even if you're not seeing a particular show.

2 MUSÉE DE LA CHASSE ET DE LA NATURE

62 rue des Archives, 75003
01 53 01 92 40
www.chassenature.org
Open Tues–Sat 11am–6pm,
Wed to 9.30pm
Metro: Rambuteau
[MAP p. 180 C2]

Mysterious, thrilling and hilarious, this collection transcends its 'stuffed animal' museum brief to create a seductive fantasy world. Exploring our own elemental role as predator, and occasional prey, a vast taxidermy collection, along with paintings, drawings and sculptures, is spread across two 17th-century townhouses. The displays are set in a series of theatrically decorated, richly historic rooms, sometimes in cabinets, but often in startling places. Artworks depict each species type, and there are tools of the trade too: falcon's hoods, horses' bridles and weapons. Seasonal shows care of contemporary artists, say French superstar Sophie Calle, add yet another layer of wonder. As do permanent installations – spot the Jeff Koons' puppy nonchalantly propped on a mantel, look up for the enchanting feathered owl ceiling by Belgian artist Jan Fabre.

POCKET TIP
The Seine's linden-tree lined islands Île Saint-Louis and Île de la Cité are ripe for a wander with historic streets and Insta-famous cafes.

POCKET TIP

For more of Serge Bensimon's design aesthetic, head to Gallery S.Bensimon, just around the corner (111 rue de Turenne, closed Sunday).

3 BENSIMON HOME AUTOUR DU MONDE

8 rue des Francs-Bourgeois, 75003
01 42 77 06 08
www.bensimon.com
Open Mon–Sat 11am–7pm, Sun 1.30–7pm
Metro Chemin-Vert
[MAP p. 181 D3]

Le *tennis Bensimon*, the coloured cotton canvas plimsoll synonymous with casual French style, were launched in 1978 by the brothers Bensimon, a creative powerhouse who have gone on to work their signature insouciance into a whole Bensimon-branded lifestyle. This, their original Marais homewares shop, carries a covetable collection of objects and furniture sourced from international designers and artists, all displayed alongside their iconic, indispensible shoes. Clothing includes both unstructured blazers and military-style jackets, chinos and shorts, which vary only in colourway from year to year, as well as seasonal shirts, tunics and dresses. They stock a large variety of bags and luggage and very well-priced candles and perfume. The ever-elegant Charlotte Bensimon, wife of co-founder Serge, is often on hand to advise. There's a clothing-focused branch a few shops down at number 12.

4 MERCI

111 boulevard Beaumarchais,
75003
01 42 77 00 33
www.merci-merci.com
Open Mon–Sat 10am–7pm
Metro St-Sébastien-Froissart
[MAP p. 181 E2]

At cult concept shop Merci there's always a heart fluttering moment when you catch sight of their mascot, a red Fiat 500 that guards the inner courtyard entrance. Temper your excitement while taking in their latest thematic collaborations (anything from patchwork knickers made with recycled Italian silk to artisanal cleaning products) filling the dramatic double height entrance, then it's up, down and around the sprawling three ex-factory floors. Here is Paris' most seductive, and ever changing, collection of local fashion labels (say Parisians Swindens and Isabel Marant or Spanish Masscob or Lebor Gabala) for men and women along with accessories, jewellery, homewares, furniture, linen and stationery. House label T-shirts, totes, scarves, pendants and leather satchels are well priced and there's a great range of basic French homewares downstairs. If you're *really* here to shop, make luggage space for the Merci-brand linen or crumpled cotton sheets (they have a tactile appeal like no other).

POCKET TIP

Post-purchase hunger pangs? Fabulously fresh salad plates, rustic cakes and organic wine await in the beautifully calm garden facing Pottager restaurant downstairs at Merci.

33

5 OLIVIA CLERGUE

6 rue du Parc Royal, 75003
06 72 73 54 92
www.oliviaclergue.com
Open Tues–Fri 12pm–7pm,
Sat 2–7pm
Metro Chemin-Vert
[MAP p. 181 D2]

Trained as a sculptor and from a stellar creative lineage (father Lucien was a Magnum photographer and Pablo Picasso her godfather), Arles-born Olivia Clergue's bags and accessories are timeless and elegant with an artist's eye for volume and detail. All are made in the French region of Anjou, and utilise traditional artisan knowledge, while taurillon, nappa and caviar leather is sourced from environmentally friendly French or Italian suppliers. Shapes run from playful satchel bags, beautiful girlish circular styles to super roomy, ridiculously practical totes. Embellishments are absent or kept to a minimum: rhythmic studs, a fringe or the pop of mix-and-match colourways. Breathe easy as the shop has friendly, passionate staff, prices are moderate given the made-in-France quality and there's canvas or straw totes and purses if you're not in serious bag purchasing mode.

POCKET TIP
Paris has more famous and historic department stores but I always recommend the Marais' BHV.

6 OFR

20 rue Dupetit-Thouars, 75003
Open Mon–Sat 10am–8pm,
Sun 2–7pm
Metro Temple
[MAP p. 178 C4]

This bookshop and its gallery space, tucked down an art-clad corridor, often feels more akin to a neighbourhood drop-in centre than a bookshop. Alexandre and Marie Thumerelle – a brother-and-sister team – have been sourcing the city's most interesting collection of printed matter for almost two decades, while showing an edgy line-up of international and local artists, both well established and emerging, in their sparse backroom gallery. The stacks of art and architecture books, densely packed magazine stands and jumble of artisanal accessories, from homewares to scarves, T-shirts and leather sandals, lure in casual passers-by and can hold you hostage for hours. Once you're in, count on being back for more, with a packed weekly calendar of openings, launches and events in the evenings, which all spill out onto the pretty street outside.

POCKET TIP

Galerie Perrotin shows stellar international contemporary artists; their bookshop and nearby Yvon Lambert bookshop stock artbooks and limited edition posters.

7 MARCHÉ DES ENFANTS ROUGES

39 rue de Bretagne, 75003
Open Tues–Thurs 8.30am–1pm
& 4–7.30pm, Sat 8.30am–1pm
& 4–8pm, Sun 8.30am–2pm
Metro Temple
[MAP p. 178 C4]

At over four hundred years old, this covered market is the oldest in Paris (its poetic name harks back even further, to the days when an orphanage occupied the site and its little charges were clad all in red). Haut-Marais locals do stock up on flowers and fresh produce here, but Enfants Rouges comes into its own for a mix-and-match bite. Grab Afro-Antillean curries and accra (fish fritters), wonderful Moroccan tajines, couscous and pastries or an all-organic roast and vegetable gratin plate. The market's most popular stall is Japanese, although the Italian enoteca also has its fans. It's possibly the most charming of Paris' covered markets, with courtyard seating for summer and snug stools and booths for winter.

POCKET TIP
While you're here, browse Fabien Breuvart's vintage photography shop (rue Charlot), or, in mid-May or November, look out for the brocante stalls on rue de Bretagne.

POCKET TIP

Excellent coffee, cakes and big brunches are at Fragments (76 rue des Tournelles, 3rd); Boot (19 rue du Pont aux Choux, 3rd) and Loustic (40 rue Chapon, 3rd).

8 CARBÓN PARIS

14 rue Charlot, 75003
01 42 72 49 12
www.carbonparis.com
Open Tues–Sun 12pm–2.30pm,
Tues–Sat 7pm–2am
Metro Filles du Calvaire
[MAP p. 181 D1]

Walking into Carbón feels like you're suddenly on holiday, even if you already are. Big windows, walls of rough sandstone, natural leather and hand-hewn wood banquettes along with a forest of tumbling foliage, bring a relaxed, enticing sensuality to this cafe. The informality continues with mix-and-match small dishes and generous share plates. Everything is cooked via a wood fire or smoking – elemental, yes, but also creative and sophisticated. A pollock and peach carpaccio is topped with fragrant verbena and fresh almonds; poached oysters come with white asparagus and nettles. The large meat or seafood plates are also spectacular. There's a hidden bar below, where the well-priced cocktail menu might offer up a daiquiri made with rum infused with charred pineapple skin, black molasses and lemon or lower alcohol aperitifs. Wines are all natural, mostly French but with some nice Italians and Austrians, including cult vintners Gut Oggau: trust the staff's picks.

9 GRAND CAFÉ TORTONI

45 rue de Saintonge, 75003
01 42 72 28 92
Open daily 11am–7pm
Metro Filles du Calvaire
[MAP p. 178 C4]

This evocative, fragrant sanctuary has an old-world cafe atmosphere that you rarely find elsewhere in Paris and there's also a tangible sense of neighbourly welcome, with locals dropping in for mid-morning espressos and a chat. Ramdane Touhami and Victoire de Taillac are known for their storytelling magic (from Cire de Trudon candles to current skincare line, l'Officine Universelle Buly). Here, they've reimagined a famous historical cafe, the first place to serve ice-cream in Paris, and haunt of writers Stendhal and Balzac. Swathes of deep red marble and cherry-hued woodwork set a beautiful stage; coffee is made on a handsome vintage espresso machine, served in jewel-coloured demitasse cups, with a refreshing water and little biscotti. There'll be a voluptuous fruit tart to tempt, as well as a cabinet of onigiri (Japanese rice pyramids) in unexpected flavours. Post-coffee, sniff and sample handcreams, lotions and oils at the Buly 1803 counter.

POCKET TIP
For picnic supplies and great gourmet present buying, Maison Plisson (93 boulevard Beaumarchais, 3rd) is the city's most stylish épicerie.

10 VINS DES PYRÉNÉES & LE 1905

25 rue Beautreillis, 75004
01 42 72 64 94
www.vinsdespyrenees.com
Open daily 8am–2pm
Metro St-Paul
[MAP p. 181 E4]

Are you longing for historic Paris surrounds but have a desire to eat smart, unfussy neo-bistro dishes too? This storied restaurant is for you. New owner Florian Cadiou's makeover has kept beautiful original features like the mosaic floors, while expanses of graphic floral fabrics and deep forest tones reflect current interior trends. The menu is less trad bistrot-a-vin, more mod Mediterranean comfort food: think lamb croquettes, grilled sardines with zucchini and citrus or spiced Vendée duck with haricots. Quality produce and an impressive, if expensive, wine list, means it's smart enough for a special occasion but also somewhere you'd be happy plonking down for a quick truffled croque-monsieur and a Pinot after a day's Marais shopping. Upstairs, in what was once the original owner's rambling apartment, accessed by a discreet side stair, you'll find Le 1905. Here you can take subtly flavoured, ancient seeming cocktails, at a tiny table or in deep chairs, or out on the Marais' most sought-after terrace.

POCKET TIP
Rue Beautreillis is where rock star Jim Morrison lived and (supposedly) died, and poet Charles Baudelaire and muse Jeanne Duval were shacked up a century earlier.

11 AU PETIT FER À CHEVAL

30 rue Vieille du Temple, 75004
01 42 72 47 47
Open daily 8am–2am
Metro Hôtel de Ville, St-Paul
[MAP p. 180 C3]

Favoured by locals and fashion types, but nowhere near as sceney or boozy as nearby institutions La Perle or Le Pick Clops, this ridiculously charming hole-in-the-wall possesses what might be the city's smallest zinc bar. The diminutive horseshoe (hence the bar's name) is an affable place to pull up a stool, sip a kir Royale and stare into the tain-stained 100-year-old mirrors, or, if you're quick, nab one of the handful of terrace tables and watch the Marais throng pass by. Wines by the glass are well-priced if non-descript, and if you're hungry, there's very generous plates of Comte or charcuterie, terrine stuffed baguettes or simple salads. As per the Paris of legends long past, the black and white clad barmen are sometimes your beaming best friend, other times, glum and surly (and sometimes both in one drink order). If you've had your apéro and aren't keen to move on, surprise – there's a restaurant squirrelled away at the rear, serving traditional French food until late.

POCKET TIP
For Hôtel de Ville and Eiffel Tower views, head to summer-only rooftop bar Le Perchoir Marais (37 rue de la Verrerie).

LEFT BANK, 5TH, 6TH, 13TH & 15TH

The Left Bank's Latin Quarter (5th) is where the Romans first settled in the 1st-century BC, although the 'Latin' was coined later, to reflect the Latin-speaking academics of its booming medieval universities. It's still a student haunt with the university of the Sorbonne occupying much of its western flank and the lush Jardin des Plantes (botanic gardens) and stately Panthéon adding to its charms.

Nearby St-Germain-des-Prés (6th) was a byword for bohemia for much of the last century, the one-time haunt of Satre and De Beauvoir, and later Serge and Jane, and the scene of street fighting in 1968. Now it's known for the antique dealers that line the rue Bonaparte and Quai Malaquais, luxury label flagships down boulevard Saint-Germain and scores of small shops and artisans clustered in the streets between. Legendary cafes Les Deux Magots and Café de Flore draw tourists though still keep their bookish old-timers, while the Jardin du Luxembourg is a green, serene piece of Parisian paradise.

To the west, the 13th's wide, wide boulevards of Gobelins, Chinatown and the Place d'Italie's shopping malls and office blocks, and once bohemian Montparnasse (15th) can make you feel like you're no longer in Paris.

Metro: Odéon, Saint-Germain-des-Prés, Jussieu, Luxembourg, Quai de la Gare

↳ *Archways of the rue de Vaugirard, Paris' longest street*

SIGHTS
1. La Grande Mosquée de Paris
2. Monnaie de Paris
3. Musée Bourdelle

SHOPPING
4. Diptyque
5. Le Bonbon au Palais

SHOPPING & EATING
6. Shakespeare and Company

EATING
7. La Guinguette d'Angèle
8. Le Felicità
9. Café de la Nouvelle Mairie
10. Breizh Café Odeon

DRINKING
11. Lapérouse Bar

1 LA GRANDE MOSQUÉE DE PARIS

2 bis Place du Puits de l'Ermite, 75005
01 45 35 97 33
www.mosqueedeparis.net
Open Sat–Thurs 9am–12pm & 2–6pm, Fri worship only
Metro Maubert-Mutualité
[MAP p. 184 B2]

Paris' beautiful early 20th-century mosque was built as a tribute to the many Muslim soldiers who fought for France in World War I. Its classical sculpted arcades recall the medieval Alhambra in Granada, and its characteristic green-and-white-tiled minaret towers above the surrounding neighbourhood. The internal gardens are particularly pretty in spring and summer but it's a serene and transporting place to visit any time of year. As a functioning mosque, prayer rooms are limited to those here to worship, but you're otherwise free to wander the beautiful libraries, contemplation rooms and quiet corridors. A separate entrance leads to its attached **salon de thé** (tea salon), another labyrinth of jewel-coloured rooms and tiled inner courtyards. While away an afternoon with thé à la menthe (mint tea), or a superbly sweet-sour citronade and nutty, fragrant Maghrebi pastries or tagines and couscous if you need lunch.

POCKET TIP
The mosque's traditional hammam (bath house) is also here; book ahead for treatments and check the male and female time slots online.

POCKET TIP
The nearby Institut du Monde Arabe (IMA), with beautiful contemporary architecture by Jean Nouvel, showcases a wonderful collection of Islamic art and has a rooftop restaurant.

2 MONNAIE DE PARIS

11 Quai de Conti, 75006
01 40 46 56 66
www.monnaiedeparis.fr
Open Tues–Sun 11am–7pm,
Wed to 9pm
Metro Pont Neuf, Mabillon
[MAP p. 183 B2]

Coins were minted here until 1973, in what is the world's oldest continuously-running mint, dating back to 864 BC, and now it's also known for its extraordinary contemporary art program. International artists are invited to install large-scale sculptural works in opulent neoclassical salons that span an entire floor. Rarely slammed with queues, it's a lovely space to wander among works by the likes of Grayson Perry, Maurizio Cattelan, Thomas Schutte or Subodh Gupta, with sweeping views across the Seine only adding to the appeal. Commemorative issues and official medals are, charmingly, still produced here too and downstairs there's an interactive museum of coins, the **Musée du 11 Conti**. The Michelin-starred restaurant is care of Guy Savoy, but there's also **Frappé by BLOOM cafe**, with a fresh, simple menu. Excellent cocktails and bar snacks are also served from Thursday to Saturday.

POCKET TIP
Taste test to find your favourite macaron on the Macaron Mile (rue Bonaparte), with Ladurée at no. 21 and Pierre Hermé at no. 72.

3 MUSÉE BOURDELLE

8 rue Antoine Bourdelle, 75015
01 49 54 73 73
www.bourdelle.paris.fr
Open Tues–Sat 10am–6pm
Metro Montparnasse-
Bienvenüe, Falguière
[MAP p. 182 A3]

Seek out this museum, dedicated to early 20th-century sculptor (and Rodin prodigy) Antoine Bourdelle, and squirrelled away up in a residential part of Monparnasse (15th). Come for its temporary shows, such as its recent Balenciaga frockbuster or Rodin and Giacometti survey, but it's the intimacy and intense presence of his dark-wooded atelier that will truly enchant. Its original glass roof, viewing mezzanine and scattered molds and worktables are much as they would have been in Monparnasse's creative heyday. A vast cathedral-like space was constructed in the 1960s to house the Bourdelle's most monumental casts, including spectacular reliefs from the Théâtre des Champs-Élysées. A 1988 extension by architect Christian de Portzamparc now contains most of the bronzes. The lush gardens are also filled with sculptures, including the ivy-clad haven of peace that is the interior courtyard (look out for the bronze of poetess Sapho, on her solitary rock).

POCKET TIP
Hexagone Café (121 rue du Château), five minutes' walk from Gare Montparnasse, serves lovingly made espresso and excellent drip filter.

4 DIPTYQUE

34 boulevard Saint Germain, 75005
01 43 26 77 44
www.diptyqueparis.fr
Open Mon–Sat 10am–7pm
Metro Maubert-Mutalité, Cardinal Lemoine
[MAP p. 184 B1]

'Flagship' is synonymous with doorman-fronted flash mini-cities, but not so at Diptyque's HQ, which still occupies the original shop where it all began in 1961. Whether you're after a well-priced perfume roll-on, mini travel candle or covet something larger, it's a decidedly intimate affair. Eclectic carpet, decorative wallpaper, pretty painted finishes and objects make exploring the perfumes, home fragrance and skincare a gorgeous experience. Interiors and window displays honour founders Christiane Gautrot, Desmond Knox-Leet and Yves Coueslant's spirit of creative curiosity and sensory wonder. Look out for their commemorative Collection 34, named for this very shop and created by capturing its rich olfactory essence. Blond wood, crushed leaves, spices of the souk and countless other elements make for a fittingly elegant, intriguing fragrance. Wrapping here is a flight of fancy: your gift (or gift to self) will be decked out in a riot of rainbow tissue.

POCKET TIP
Buy discounted French skincare lines (La Roche-Posay, Nuxe, Bioderma) at parapharmacies City Pharma (6th) or the smaller, but calmer Pharmacie Montorgueil Parispharma (2nd).

5 LE BONBON AU PALAIⱭ

19 rue Monge, 75005
01 78 56 15 72
www.bonbonsaupalais.fr
Open Tues–Sat 10.30am–
7.30pm
Metro Maubert-Mutalité,
Cardinal Lemoine
[MAP p. 184 B1]

This 'palace of sweets' is a tour of the tastes and smells of childhood for its French customers, with everything you can see in the jam-packed shop sourced from traditional confiseur (confectioner) workshops from every region of France. Georges Marques had a lifelong desire to open such a place and his sweet school-room decor and friendly air add to the nostalgia his wares summon. Vintage apothecary-style jars are filled with cocoa-dusted pralines, crystallised flowers of all description, caramels and pâtes de fruit. But if the ability to make rational choices alludes you, the pretty pastel guimauve – fragrant, pillowy marshmallow blocks from Bayonne – in flavours such as fleur d'oranger (orange blossom), poire (pear) and cerise (cherry), are, as you'll discover, the best in Paris – and a wise, if addictive, choice. Vegans and vegetarians will find many things that are made without gelatin or egg whites – just ask.

POCKET TIP

The Paris catacombs, an extensive underground ossuary dating back to the 1780s, is a fascinating, morbid and eerily beautiful place to visit.

6 SHAKESPEARE AND COMPANY

37 rue de la Bûcherie, 75005
01 43 25 40 93
www.shakespeareand
company.com
Open Mon–Sun 10am–11pm
(bookshop), Mon–Sun
9.30am–7.30pm (cafe)
Metro Saint Michel Notre
Dame, Cluny la Sorbonne
[MAP p. 183 C3]

George Whitman's left bank
bookshop was bequeathed
to daughter Sylvia after his
death in 2011 and, apart from
some behind-the-scenes
modernisation, it remains the
rich, rambling, bohemian hub
that's nurtured, nourished
and often housed writers and
readers since the Beat era.
And, yes, there are books to
be bought among its delightful
warren of upstairs downstairs
rooms, not just a mythological
back story to soak in; a
thoughtfully curated section on
Paris – including history, food,
politics, city life – should be
a first stop. Joining this busy
bookish hub in recent years
is a cafe. Its busy riverside
locale (note spectacular view
of Notre Dame), mean it's not
exactly a place for writerly
contemplation, though the
coffee, from Montmartre roaster
Café Lomi, is good enough to
warrant a visit alone. As are
the cakes, mostly vegetarian
lunch dishes and English teas.

POCKET TIP

Shakespeare and
Company's antiquarian
collection (closed Sunday &
Monday) is a bibliophile's
delight, with covetable
first editions by the likes
of DH Lawrence and
James Joyce.

POCKET TIP
The Jardin du Luxembourg (6th) is beautiful and historic; its little forest and orchard, network of sculptures and famous pond can occupy an entire afternoon.

7 LA GUINGUETTE D'ANGÈLE

6 rue de Tournon, 75006
09 81 81 05 65
www.laguinguettedangele.com
Open Tues–Sat 12pm–5pm
Metro Odéon
[MAP p. 183 A3]

Join academics and stylish young families for a vegetable-packed lunchbox, sandwich or soups, with tablecloths and fresh flowers making it feel more special than your average cafe lunch. Angèle Ferreux Maeght is one of Paris' healthy eating pioneers, with cookbooks and both a take-away in the 1st and a small cafe by the 11th's Square Gardette. This latest, and largest, project occupies the basement and beautiful courtyard of **Bonpoint**'s flagship shop, and her sweet, rustic styling and daytime treats are a lovely complement to the much-coveted childrenswear above. Maeght honed her passion for cooking in California and Australia, but everything on the menu is done with an unmistakable French flair and extraordinary organic ingredients. You can also pop in and pick up a little gouter (snack), such as a matcha cookie or coconut riz au lais (rice pudding) before heading to the Jardin du Luxembourg for a picnic. All is gluten free, there's vegan options, and groceries.

8 LE FELICITÀ

5 Parvis Alan Turing, 75013
www.lafelicita.fr
Open Mon–Tues 12.15pm–
2.30pm, Mon–Fri 6–11pm,
Sat & Sun 12pm–11pm
Metro Chevaleret
[MAP p. 190 B4]

Station F, a start-up hub of football pitch proportions, is the very embodiment of President Macron's new entrepreneurial France, and its 'canteen', across the tracks from the veritable Bibliotheque Nationale, is very much the 'new Paris' too. At 4500m², Le Felicità is touted as the largest restaurant in Europe, brought to you by the Big Mamma group whose mass-Italianisation mission began at East Mamma in Bastille (and has continued apace with Pink Mamma in Pigalle and several other locations). It's noisy, occasionally frenetic, with Paris' young and photogenic wandering about under huge balloons, through indoor forests and packing out the picnic tables or train carriage seating. Join them for pizzas – all organic and authentically simple – Piedmontese style ravioli, spaghetti with tomato and ricotta or truffles and cream. If you're not dining, groaning burratta and proscuitto platters can help you sop up the endless Negronis and Aperol spritzes.

POCKET TIP

Behind the Place d'Italie, The Butte-aux-Cailles' (13th) village-like enclave of cobbled streets and ivy-clad townhouses is known for its boisterous bars and cheap restaurants.

POCKET TIP

Seine-side, the Quai de Austerlix has its party-boats, a summer 'beach' and its all-weather bars.

9 CAFÉ DE LA NOUVELLE MAIRIE

19 rue des Fossés Saint-Jacques, 75005
01 44 07 04 41
Open Mon–Fri 8am–12am
Metro Place Monge,
Cardinal Lemoine
[MAP p. 184 A2]

Just by the Panthéon and overlooking the Place de l'Estrapade fountain, this neighbourhood favourite and its sunny terrace pushes all the classic Paris-bistro buttons. Staff, in their cordial, non-committal way, are reassuringly, well, Parisian. Look beyond the signage and the dark wood chairs and you'll see a keen mid-century eye behind many of the pieces strewn about. Look again and you'll notice the well-priced wines by the glass are mostly natural and all from small estates (if you're feeling serious about tasting, go straight to their huge list, which features multiple vintages from their favourite vignerons). Food too is straightforward, comforting but refined: the œufs mayonnaise are organic, the fish rillettes come topped with coriander; and mains like roast veal or pan-crisped fish come on beds of tender grilled vegetables or warm salads. If you're just in the neighbourhood for coffee, it's faultless, but not fussed over.

POCKET TIP
Left Bankers do their daily produce shop at the pretty Marché rue Mouffetard (5th), while on Sundays they make for organic-only Marché Biologique Raspail (6th).

10 BREIZH CAFÉ ODEON

1 rue de l'Odéon, 75006
01 42 49 34 73
www.breizhcafe.com
Open Mon–Fri 11.30am–11pm,
Sat–Sun from 10am
Metro Odéon
[MAP p. 181 D2]

If you're hankering for crêpes, try this marriage of Brittany's rich produce – buckwheat, salted caramel, cider, seaweed – and Japanese finesse. Queues are long at the Marais original, but this airy and calm space has a sunny terrace and takes reservations. Gallettes made from freshly milled buckwheat are crisped in the best butter; they nod to tradition (Basque ham, fried egg and espelette pepper or smoked herring and potato) or get inventive ('maki'-style rolled gallettes, filled with, say, scrambled eggs, Comté, artichokes and wakame from Saint-Malo). Oysters from Cancale fill a front counter and there's langoustines, pork belly plates and cheese. Dessert crêpes can be matched with Bourdier butter and sugar or try the ice-cream, best enjoyed in an earthy Breton trio of buckwheat, salted caramel and buttermilk. There's lovely regional wines but you're all but obliged to drink cider, with a staggering number of options, from dry and minerally to rich, pink and fruity.

POCKET TIP

The traditional antiques shops were once the main lure of St-Germaine-des-Pres' rue Jacob (6th), but today it's also lined with both international labels and independent French designers.

55

11 LAPÉROUƧE BAR

51 Quai des Grands Augustins,
75006
01 43 26 68 04
www.laperouse.com
Open Mon–Sat 7pm–1am
Metro Pont-Neuf, St-Michel
Notre Dame
[MAP p. 183 B2]

Lapérouse's interior quirk was famed even as the newest place on the block in 1766, and the bar's kooky ramble of Persian-rug strewn nooks and acres of velvet upholstery has stood the test of time. Legend has it that the scratches on the many mirrors of Lapérouse's intimate salons were made by canny filles de joie (ladies of doubtful reputation) testing out their newly gifted diamonds (or more accurately, testing out the viability of their suitors). Realist and Romantic writers Emile Zola, George Sand and Victor Hugo later lent the place intellectual cred, though whether or not they were better behaved is anyone's guess. Pull up a chaise-longue as the Veuve Clicquot flows. Or ply through the cocktail menu, which has recently been rocketed into the 21st century, with a Plaza Athénée alumni turning out drinks named after various Left Bank ghosts; as well as on-point whisky sours and a play on former local Serge Gainsbourgh's particular poison, the daiquiri.

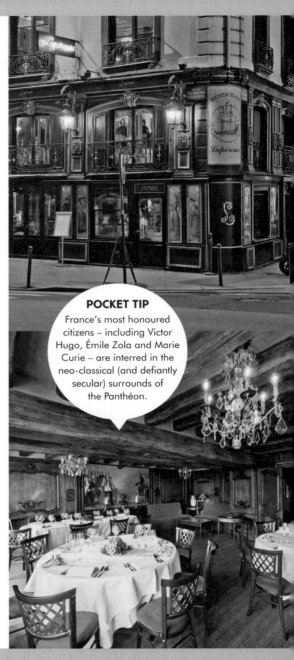

POCKET TIP
France's most honoured citizens – including Victor Hugo, Émile Zola and Marie Curie – are interred in the neo-classical (and defiantly secular) surrounds of the Panthéon.

EIFFEL TOWER & CHAMPS-ÉLYSÉES, 7TH, 8TH & 16TH

Welcome to Paris' rarified west. Aristocratic to its very core, the 7th is home to some of the city's grandest civic institutions and iconic destinations – the Eiffel Tower, the museums of Les Invalides, the Impressionist-filled Musée d'Orsay (*see* p. 61) and the Musée Rodin (*see* p. 60). It's also a precinct with Michelin-starred dining and luxury shopping, but you'll find street markets and more affordable cafes too.

Across the river, the 8th's tree-lined Champs-Élysées comes into its own on La Fête Nationale (Bastille Day) parades and Tour de France finishes, framed by Napoléon's Arc de Triomphe. Shopping, or at least a spot of lèche-vitrine (window shopping), though is better in the nearby Golden Triangle, delineated by avenue George V, avenue Montaigne and avenue des Champs-Élysées. There's also an impressive concentration of cultural riches here too, including the Palais de Tokyo (*see* p. 62), and the fantastic collections and temporary shows of the Grand and Petit Palais.

The sprawling mostly residential 16th, its nickname 'le seiziéme' synonymous with wealth, prestige and power – is also home to Roland Garros Stadium and the stunning Fondation Louis Vuitton on its far green edge.

Metro: Varenne, Sèvres-Babylone, Alma-Marceau, Iéna, Concorde, George V

→ *Palais du Tokyo in the 16th*

1 MUSÉE RODIN

77 rue de Varenne, 75007
01 44 18 61 10
www.musee-rodin.fr
Open Tues–Sun 10am–5.45pm
Metro Varenne, Invalides
[MAP p. 182 A1]

We have the German writer
Rainer Maria Rilke to thank for
this magnificent museum. It
was he who, when employed
as the great sculptor's
secretary, spotted the potential
of the tumble-down Hôtel
Biron, as only a poet might.
Rodin went on to live, love
and, most of all, work in the
sprawling mansion for the
rest of his life and it's been a
dedicated museum since 1919,
two years after his death. After
a glamourous, high-tech and
respectful refurb a few years
back, it's still a space that's so
redolent of his genius, to be
near overwhelming. A maze of
splendid rooms display Rodin's
sculptures, many of them will
be familiar, many a surprise.
They're joined by maquettes
and models, his extraordinary
'assemblages' of Greek and
Roman antiquities, and the
viscerally affecting work of
his ill-fated lover and protégé,
Camille Claudel. Don't miss the
dimly-lit corridor that secrets
a series of Rodin's startlingly
erotic drawings. Contemporary
shows honouring his legacy
are shown in a new annex
and there's a fantastic
bookshop there too.

POCKET TIP
Leave time to
wander Rodin's sculpture
garden at the Musée
Rodin. It's a national
historical monument
in its own right.

2 MUSÉE D'ORSAY

1 rue de la Légion d'Honneur,
75007
www.musee-orsay.fr
Open Tues–Sun 9.30am–6pm,
Thurs until 9pm
Metro Solférino
[MAP p. 175 F4]

This museum, housed in
a magnificent former train
station, is where you'll find the
nation's largest collection of
Impressionist art. Blockbuster
paintings by Renoir and
Monet are joined by equally
goosebump-inducing Realist
works by Manet (the game-
changing *Olympia* and *Le
déjeuner sur l'herbe* among
them) and Post-Impressionists
a-plenty, including Cezanne,
Seurat, Signac, Gauguin
and Van Gogh. While its tidy
1848 to 1914 scope makes
it far less overwhelming
than the Louvre (*see* p. 2),
it's still worth dedicating at
least a half day to visit. Don't
overlook the sensual, gentle
Nabis, including Bonnard
and Vuillard, and sublimely
kooky Symbolists such as
Puvis de Chavenne. There's
also an impressive sculpture
collection (A standout? The
touching *Small Dancer Aged
14* by Degas). The **bookshop**
is a delight, as is the **cafe**. Buy
tickets online (it's quicker),
and for discounted admission
come after 4.30pm, or 6pm
on Thursdays.

POCKET TIP

Controversial Musée
du Quai Branly houses
a phenomenal collection
of artefacts and artworks,
much of which were taken
from France's former
colonies.

3 PALAIƧ DE TOKYO

13 avenue du Président Wilson,
75016
www.palaisdetokyo.com &
www.mam.paris.fr
Open Wed–Mon 12pm–12am
(Palais de Tokyo), Tues–Sun
10am–6pm (MAM)
Metro Iéna, Alma Marceau
[MAP p. 174 B3]

One great stonking piece of
Modernist architecture houses
two museums, with two
distinct moods and works of art
that many visitors miss seeing.
On one side, the beautiful
1937 Exposition Internationale
building houses the largest
kunsthalle-style museum in
France, the Palais de Tokyo,
which bills itself as an 'anti-
museum'. A recent refit, almost
doubling the footprint, keeps
its perpetually 'in-progress'
look of steel girders and
exposed concrete. Seasonally
changing, high-profile shows
of French contemporary art are
always worth it: spectacular,
serious, and, at times, seriously
fun. There's a great made-for-
lingering cafe here too. Across
the courtyard, are the gentle
collections of the **Musée d'Art
Moderne de la Ville de
Paris (MAM)**. This might just
become your own little Parisian
secret: somewhere you can
commune in peace with a
Pierre Bonnard (or a Picasso,
Matisse or Yves Klein) … no,
there's no queues or jostling
and it's free (temporary shows
are ticketed).

POCKET TIP
Chase museum overload
away with the ecstatic
chromatic overload of
Raoul Dufy's *La Fée
Electricité*, a monumental
work commissioned for
the original Palais de
Tokyo building.

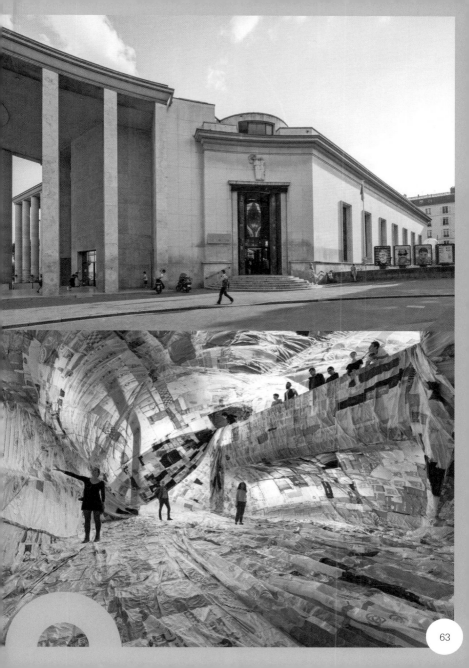

4 HOLIDAY BOILEAU

11 rue Parent de Rosan, 75016
09 67 25 56 40
www.holiday-paris.fr
Open Tues–Sat 10am–7pm
Metro Pont de Sèvres
[MAP p. 193 C3]

Is one place worth a journey to the residential reaches of the deeply bourgeois 16th? Yes! Franck Durand rescued the classic mid-century travel magazine *Holiday* from oblivion in 2014 and has more recently turned his creative direction genius to a clothing label for men and women of the same name. Italian tailoring, subtle, stylish colourways and vintage inspiration from the original *Holiday* archive makes for pieces that scream style over trends. This light, pared-back shop, sitting at the base of a beautiful 20th-century apartment building, has the full collection, including colourful cult sweatshirts, reclaimed denim jackets, key chains, and bright, sturdy totes. The goods are surrounded by paintings, photos, books, magazines and decorative objects that only an eye like Durand might choose. Durand is also restoring **Village Boileau's** early 20th-century workers' cottages and artisan ateliers, and a wander around the surrounding streets is a pleasure. Also, on nearby avenue de Versaille, you'll find the **Holiday café**, a perfect locals-who-brunch spot.

POCKET TIP
Phillippe d'Orleans' 1778 Parc Monceau makes for an easy, idyllic escape, with its elegant English-style follies, lake and vegetable gardens.

POCKET TIP

Late-night shopping urges *and* burger cravings can both be met at the Publicis Drugstore (avenue des Champs-Elysées), where its shop and restaurants are open until 2am.

5 TRADING MUSEUM COMME DES GARÇONS

54 rue du Faubourg Saint-Honoré, 75008
01 42 65 91 19
Open Mon–Sat 11am–7pm
Metro Madeleine
[MAP p. 175 E2]

Paris is a city that makes, curates and propagates fashion trends. Trading Museum is one of those dizzyingly category defying mash-ups where those trends are on show daily, and where designer Rei Kawakubo creates a world where there is 'a reason and story' behind everything that you see. Here, 'just looking' for inspiration, rather than mere shopping, is highly encouraged, if not the entire point. Nestled in a back courtyard of the Comme des Garçons' mothership compound, here fashion meets art, demi-couture meets street, past vintage meets its future self and the signature perfume is designed with notes of sticky tape and fake flowers. They also host installations and seasonal artist collaborations, but if you are wondering what they do actually sell, you can pick up caps, oversized tees and hoodies from Russian skater brand Paccbet, jewellery from Simone Rocha, doll-like frocks from Molly Goddard, and a trainer collab with whoever's the next Gosha Rubchinsky.

6 LE BON MARCHÉ

24 & 38 rue de Sèvres, 75007
01 44 39 80 00
www.lebonmarche.com
Open Mon–Wed & Sat 10am–
8pm, Thurs–Fri to 9pm (Le Bon
Marché), Mon–Sat 8.30am–
9pm (Grand Épicerie)
Metro Sèvres-Babylone
[MAP p. 182 B2]

Designed by Louis-Charles
Boileau and Gustave Eiffel,
no less, this most glamourous
of the grands magasins
(department stores) was
launched in 1852 to be 'a new
kind of store that would thrill
all the senses'. The current
interior is the work of superstar
designer Andree Putman,
whose oh-so-'80s remodel is
even more in fashion today
than it was when unveiled.
From the vast perfume section
to big name luxury labels to
easy Parisian go-tos like
Majestic and Carven, there's
retail thrills-a-plenty. Next
door, the Grand Épicerie
has a rooftop cafe and four
upmarket grocery departments
to wander – 'basic, traditional,
rare and ultra-sophisticated'
comestibles; seasonal fresh
produce; over 2000 wines in
a basement cellar; and house
kitchens that stock pâtisserie,
chocolaterie and boulangerie
counters as well as picnic or
hotel room-ready dishes. Come
the season, visit for magical
Christmas windows and a
delightful decoration shop.

POCKET TIP
Ogle the Eiffel Tower while
you wander among the
produce stalls of Marché
Saxe-Breteuil (7th, Thursday
and Saturday) or head to
Coutume Babylone (7th)
for great coffee.

7 LA LAITERIE ƎAINTE-CLOTILDE

64 rue de Bellechasse, 75007
01 45 51 74 61
www.lalaiteriesainteclotilde.fr
Open Mon—Fri 12pm—2.30pm,
8—11pm, Sat 8—11pm
Metro Solférino, Rue du Bac
[MAP p. 182 B1]

A relaxed and welcoming
retreat in a precinct that can
be anything but, this sweet
little space packed with school
chairs and wee wooden tables
still has the shopfront feel of
the dairy it once was. The small
kitchen offers up thoughtful,
tasty dishes for far less than
the re-heated fare you'll
get at many neighbouring
tourist traps and the service
is genuinely friendly and
passionate about what's on
your plate. The fixed price
lunch menu also allows you to
choose across all the à la carte
dishes. These will be simple,
say, a cold soup in summer, or
ravioli in winter, a good steak
with sauté potatoes or cod
with a nori-topped gribiche.
Desserts too are unpretentious:
fresh pineapple with ginger
and lime or a rich chocolate
cake. A neatly curated wine list
is smart enough to please the
suits at lunch and well-heeled
locals at night, but well priced
enough to linger with an extra
glass or two.

POCKET TIP

For a late-night classic
tartare or steak-frites,
head to La Maison de
l'Aubrac (37 rue Marbeuf,
8th) who open at least
until 1am and onto dawn
from Wednesday to
Saturday.

8 L'AMI JEAN

27 rue Malar, 75007
01 47 05 86 89
www.lamijean.fr
Open Tues–Sat 12pm–2pm,
7–11pm
Metro Invalides, La Tour-
Maubourg
[MAP p. 174 C4]

This 1931 bistro's accent is
Basque rather than Parisian
and with owner Stéphane
Jégo himself hailing from the
west coast, and at the helm
for two decades, there's a
lovely sense of continuity.
Don't be fooled by the dark
wooden booths and delightfully
lived-in vibe though – this is
not budget dining. That said,
the huge four-course business
lunch is good value indeed for
around €30; and a long lunch
or late-sitting dinner under
its vintage storybook Paris
murals and chandeliers is an
occasion to remember. If you're
lucky, the parmesan soup will
be on – an unctuous, high-
umami concoction poured over
crisped croutons of country
bread. Shared mains, such as
a slow-cooked leg of lamb or
a boned wild hare with a bed
of jus-infused vegetables or a
creamy purée (mash), are also
outstanding. And the creamy
vanilla-flecked rice pudding
is *the* dessert to order. Wines
too are small producer, if
old school posh, rather than
renegade natural.

POCKET TIP
Two giant boats are
docked side by side in the
7th: Le Flow has a small
concert hall below decks
with live music; Rosa
Bonheur has DJs and
a huge weekend
party scene.

9 LE/ GRAND/ VERRE/

13 avenue du Président Wilson,
75016
01 85 53 03 61
www.quixotic-projects.com
Open daily 12pm–2.30am,
7–11pm, bar until 2am
Metro Iéna, Alma Marceau
[MAP p. 174 B3]

The Palais de Tokyo's (*see*
p. 62) newest dining room,
Les Grands Verres, is an
unabashed people pleaser.
It shares the museum's
cavernous concrete skeleton,
though the post-apocalyptic
vibe here is very much
softened by large expanses
of blond wood, rich, earthily
toned textiles and intimate,
low hanging lighting. Brought
to you by the hospitality
wunderkinds responsible
for the much-feted Le Mary
Celeste, Candelaria, Glass,
and Hero, the menu is a bold,
broad Mediterranean mix. Try
the chargrilled octopus paired
with pickled blackberries and
coriander, lamb tartare with
tahini and mint or a simple
slab of tuna served with confit
tomatoes and fried capers. If
you're dining with a group,
large platters of ribeye or
smoked pork can be shared.
Cocktails are how this gang
first won Paris over, so expect
them to be great, though
the natural wines are well
chosen too.

10 CRAVAN

17 rue Jean-de-la-Fontaine, 75016
01 40 50 14 30
Open daily 8am–11pm
Metro Jasmin, Ranelagh
[MAP p. 170 B3]

POCKET TIP
The 8th and the 16th have a number of designer consignment shops, called dépôt-vente. The 16th's huge Réciproque can be found at 93 rue dela Pompe.

In opening this all-day bar-cafe, the 11th's Franck Audoux brings cocktail savvy to the staid 16th. Named for proto-Dadaist poet and pugilist, Arthur Cravan, the gorgeous, bijou space is set in an Art Nouveau treasure by Hector Guimard. Marble counters, tiles daubed with swags of roses and painted mirrors surround a zinc bar: pretty without a hint of twee. Cocktails too are ethereal, poetic plays on the classics. Audoux knows his stuff, having penned the cocktail bible *French Moderne*. The Yellow, served in an evocative stemmed cup, brings together gin, the French gentian bitters Suze and chartreuse; while the Trocadero is a negroni-like mix of vermouth, curacao and Picon, an apéritif from the north of France. French-Anglo comfort food – croque-madame sandwiches, foie gras, a plate of white asparagus, big weekend roasts – add to the home-away-from-home feel. Drop in from 8am for eggs or granola; one of the Marais' best baristas, Youssef Louanjli has decamped here, so there's perfect coffee too.

PIGALLE &
OPÉRA, 9TH

The raunchy, red light days are all but over, and
the 9th today is an arrondissement of wildly diverse
personalities, one that's currently reinventing itself by
the day. Place Pigalle, on the border of the 18th, still
has its tour buses and textbook sleaze but the hostess
bars and guitar shops of the surrounding streets are
fast disappearing, replaced by cocktail saloons, clubs
and small independent retailers. If you're looking to
party hard and well past 2am, this is the place to do
it. It occasionally won't feel like Paris, but then at that
time of the morning, it might not even seem like Planet
Earth. The 'SoPi' – south Pigalle – hipster makeover
turns grown-up on gastronomically inclined and family
friendly rue des Martyrs.

On the border of the 2nd is the high Haussmanian
Grand Boulevards where the iconic twin department
stores Galeries Lafayette and Printemps faceoff, and
you'll also find the breathtaking Opéra Garnier, the
historic home of the Opéra National de Paris. Don't
miss the unique early 19th-century architecture of the
La Nouvelle Athènes (New Athens) district on rue de
la Tour-des-Dames and the surrounding streets, once
an intellectual and creative hothouse.

Metro: Pigalle, Anvers, Barbès-Rochechouart,
Saint-Georges

→ *Rue Duperré's basketball court*

1 MUSÉE NATIONAL GUSTAVE MOREAU

14 rue de la Rochefoucauld, 75009
01 48 74 38 50
www.musee-moreau.fr
Open Wed–Mon 10am–5.15pm
Metro Saint-Georges, Notre-Dame-de-Lorette
[MAP p. 172 C4]

Moreau himself helped convert his former family home into this intimate Belle-Époque museum. His upstairs studio, infused with light from huge windows, is arranged in 19th-century 'salon hang' style, with a thousand or so oil paintings, pastels, watercolours and drawings set against oxblood red walls and beneath a Lovecraftian spiral staircase. Despite Moreau claiming to be a mere peintre d'histoire, a history painter, it's an otherworldy onslaught; his mythological themes, kinky psychodrama and intimations of abstraction feel more provocative than ever. It's good bourgeois calm down in the private quarters though, with a sea-green dining room and reception rooms housing a remarkable collection of 5th-century BC Italian ceramics that belonged to his father, plus a mawkish bedroom complete with a portrait of the artist by Degas.

PORTRAIT DE GUSTAVE MOREAU PAR LUI-MÊME

POCKET TIP
The dreamy, colourful Chagall-daubed ceilings of the Opéra Garnier are alone worth taking a guided tour (or booking tickets to the opera) to see.

75

2 MUSÉE DE LA VIE ROMANTIQUE

16 rue Chaptal, 75009
01 55 31 95 67
www.museevieromantique.
paris.fr
Open Tues–Sun 10am–6pm
Metro Saint-Georges, Blanche
[MAP p. 172 C3]

A walled, rose, wisteria and fuchsia-filled garden seems improbable in this busy part of Paris. So too does this freestanding 1830s villa, all pale pink render and eau-de-nil shutters, but it's here that you'll find a small museum dedicated to Romanticism (the one with a capital 'R'). Once the home of artist Ary Scheffer, and where fellow Romantic painters Eugene Delacroix and Ingre and musicians Liszt, Rossini and neighbour Chopin were routinely invited round to apéro. The ground floor is dedicated to writer George Sand, Chopin's lover, with a mix of her jewels and watercolours and even plaster casts of her voluptuous right arm and Chopin's delicate left hand. The attached **salon de thé** (tea salon) is a (small 'r') romantic delight. Human-scaled, fragrant and with a birdsong soundtrack, there's also a handsome wintergarden for colder days. Here Rose Carriani, of rue des Martyrs' iconic Rose Bakery, turns out some of Paris' best cakes, tarts and salads.

3 SEPT CINQ

54 rue Notre Dame de Lorette, 75009
09 83 55 05 95
www.sept-cinq.com
Open Tues–Sat 11am–8pm, Sun 2–6pm
Metro: Saint-Georges, Pigalle
[MAP p. 172 C4]

The sept (seven) and cinq (five) of the name references the 75 prefix of the Parisian postcode: yes, everything here is made in Paris and the homey space houses a huge array of things to pour over. Two young business school grads, Lorna Moquet and Audrey Gallier, opened this, their original shop in 2013 (they now also have another brimming outlet in Châtelet, where there is also a tea room). Cou De Foudre's merino scarves are sustainably manufactured and come in a huge range of wintery colours. Artisan jewellers are well represented with lots of the delicate and graphic costume styles beloved by French women to choose from, including La2l's made in the Marais bohemian baubles (Marie-Hélène Spitzer's label in French poetically sounds out as: 'she has two wings'). Well-priced wallets and cardholders from Manufacture des rigoles are crafted from fine calf leather and French linen, and there are smart passport folders from style doyenne Inès de la Fressange.

POCKET TIP

Take a peek at the 9th's historic twin grand magasins (department stores), Galeries Lafayette and Printemps, but be warned there are tour buses, bollards and nothing you won't find elsewhere.

4 PIGALLE BASKETBALL

17 rue Duperré, 75009
01 45 26 17 99
www.pigalle-paris.com
Open Mon–Fri 12pm–8pm,
Sat from 10am, Sun from 2pm
Metro Pigalle
[MAP p. 172 C3]

Dubbed the King of Pigalle, 9th born and bred designer Stéphane Ashpool fuses exacting Parisian fashion culture (his eye was honed with designers like Rick Owens and Gareth Pugh) with his quartier's vibrant street and hip hop scenes. This is Ashpool's second outlet and is dedicated to hoodies, hats and sneakers (it's opposite the basketball court where he played as a kid and now trains his own team). The global success of his Pigalle label – rap and R&B royalty Rhianna and A$AP Rocky drop by when they're in town – haven't changed the very Parisian, very hands-on feel to it all (his dancer mum may well help serve you). If you're in the market for highly crafted, it street-wear inspired menswear, head to his original decade old hub down the hill at 7 rue Henry Monnier. Whether you go high or low, it's all made to the same exacting standards: most pieces are still produced in Paris.

"FOR THE LOVE OF THE GAME"

B.P.I.G.A.L.L.E.X
K.B.B.A.S.K.E.T.H
B.C.U.B.A.L.L.O.J
G.I.G.J.Y.Q.F.U.G

POCKET TIP

The op-art blur of rue Duperré's basketball court is prime selfie territory, but you can watch local kids shoot a few hoops too.

5 BOUILLON PIGALLE

22 boulevard de Clichy, 75009
01 42 59 69 31
www.bouillonpigalle.com
Open daily 12pm–12am
Metro Pigalle
[MAP p. 172 C3]

A bouillon's mission is to feed the masses, and for years this meant saucing up cheap cuts the Les Halles butchers tossed aside, like bone marrow, to cook up a tasty bouillon – broth – from all them bones. This clamourous 300 seater is a thoroughly modern incarnation by hospitality pros. Produce quality is good, servings are large and staff are cute and affable. For those familiar with a trad French menu there will be no surprises (apart perhaps from the startlingly low prices): œuf mayonnaise, herring and potatoes, boeuf bourguignon, poulet roti (roast chicken), black pudding and purée. Order a side of frites maison (house fries), as you'll otherwise be longingly eyeing off your neighbour's. The wine carte is small, as all wine is house wine. It's served in carafes from a quart (250ml) to jeroboams and is decent and astonishingly cheap. Another thing to love: if you've missed lunch and just *must* have a steak-frites at 4pm, they won't raise an eyebrow (plus you'll skip the snaking peak-time queues).

POCKET TIP

Big name live acts play L'Olympia (9th), Bus Palladium (9th), Casino de Paris (9th) Élysée Montmartre (18th) and La Cigale (18th).

6 PETRELLE

34 rue Petrelle, 75009
01 42 82 11 02
www.petrelle.fr
Open Tues–Sat 8–10pm
Metro Anvers, Barbès-
Rochechouart
[MAP p. 173 E3]

Pop in early to make a booking and you'll probably find owner-chef-decorator Jean-Luc André, his sole waiter and the house cat, all chowing down on a staff meal as the aroma of a slow braise wafts from the kitchen. Petrelle is a timeless and particularly Parisian proposition. There's the layer-upon-layer beautiful eccentricity of the dining room itself, all tricked up by André himself. Then there's his cooking: lovingly prepared meat and fish dishes, say rabbit or sardines, from trusted suppliers, paired with his homegrown vegetables and sauced traditionally. It's supposedly the place where senior politicians take their mistresses for an inconspicuous, casual outing and possibly one of the well-priced bottles of Chablis. Whether or not that's true, see those meringues adorning the entry table? They'll definitely be proffered as a take-home treat as you contentedly bid your host *bonsoir*.

POCKET TIP

Sweet cafe and providore Marlette has good coffee and gluten-free cakes. Expect great coffee at KB Café, one of Paris' first artisan roasters.

7 ARTISAN

14 rue Bochart Saron, 75009
01 48 74 65 38
www.artisan-bar.fr
Open Tues & Wed 7pm–1am,
Thurs–Sat 7pm–2am
Metro Anvers, Pigalle
[MAP p. 173 D3]

There's nothing dark or mysterious, gimmicky or even very glam about this big-windowed bar. Instead, there's a beautiful zinc counter, extremely well-crafted cocktails and a crew of laidback locals. The list changes according to the availability of seasonal fruit and vegetables along with the mood of the bartender; wines take a backstage but what they do have is well-sourced. While the tipples, whether that's an Improved Negroni or something from their biweekly changing menu, might be the raison d'être of your visit, what comes out of the kitchen comes as a very pleasant surprise too, with some of the neighbourhood's most interesting eating. Little dishes, often plays on French classics, like a herb-strewn lamb shoulder, or Frenchified international favourites, like a tuna tataki with apple guacamole, are stylishly, prettily presented but also full of substantial, subtly paired flavours. Bonus: the kitchen is open until 11pm, sometimes midnight.

8 PILE OU FACE

4 rue de Douai, 75009
06 68 02 80 38
www.pileoufacepigalle.com
Open Mon–Sat 6pm–2am
Metro Pigalle
[MAP p. 172 C3]

Eschewing the almost de rigueur dive bar or speakeasy look and staying deliciously true to its '80s girly bar roots, Pile ou Face boasts poles (the dancing kind), plush sofas and dim-to-very dark lighting. A happy, downright convivial medium if you're toying between bar or club, they turn out well-made, not overly expensive, cocktails to a very Paris-now soundtrack of classic French hits (yes, we're talking Serge Gainsborough), Scandi electronica and nu-disco greats from Oslo's finest Todd Terje to everyone's favourite Frenchmen, Daft Punk. Live acts sometimes appear on weekends and there will, of course, be dancing. The drinks card vibe is traditional but most come with clever little twists: a G&T packs an absinthe-based punch, the Yellow Mary is made with a golden tomato puree. Whisky drinkers won't be disappointed either, with a long list and flights.

POCKET TIP
Bar hop the rue Frochot strip – Glass, Dirty Dick and Lulu White – then head to rue Jean-Baptiste Pigalle to Pigalle Country Club or L'embuscade.

POCKET TIP

Pigalle's clutch of discreet boutique boltholes – Le Pigalle, Maison Souquet, Hotel Amour and the Grand Pigalle – all have excellent bars and bar dining.

9 CARMEN

34 rue Duperré, 75009
01 45 26 50 00
www.le-carmen.fr
Open Tues–Sat 6pm–6am,
Sun to 12am
Metro Pigalle
[MAP p. 172 C3]

Named for composer Georges Bizet (well his most famous opera at least), who lived upstairs in an opulent folly dating to the 1870s, this is one atmospheric place for a big night out. Two floors each have their own music and own bars; elaborate 19th-century plasterwork, stucco, caryatids, you name it, fill both. There are over forty kinds of infused gins, ranging from simple citrus ones to those spiced with white pepper or tinged with saffron. Bar staff will suggest matching mixers, if the hour isn't too late. Cosy up with yours on a Louis sofa set within a giant birdcage. Enquire ahead or check out their Facebook page: some nights are super young, and note that on any night, while the door policy is relaxed by Parisian standards, it's no pushover either. If you're keen for the gin but not fussed about kicking on, the early evening scene – pre-midnight – is very chilled, be that round the bar or out on the large terrace in summer. Plus the drinks are cheaper.

CANAL SAINT-MARTIN & RÉPUBLIQUE, 10TH

Once known mainly for its grand twin train stations, Gare du Nord and Gare de l'Est, the 10th has, of late, become one of the city's most happening places to be. The grittily pretty Canal Saint-Martin, a still working waterway whose locks link the Seine with Paris' north-east, is the scene of impromptu picnics and public flirtations of many a young Parisian and traveller. Its plane-tree-lined banks are home to a swag of stalwart bars, like Chez Prune, and loads of newcomers, along with great independent retailers. The streets that connect the canal to the Place de la Republique, and those running up to Belleville on the other side, are filled with local life, yes, bars, cafes and restaurants, too. Among the bars, the shopping is also good: local and international favourites can be found in the easy going rue des Marseille while the rue des Chateau d'Eau has its own flourishing scene with innovative independents and vintage dealers. Booming too is the Faubourg Saint-Denis, and its Culiere Paradise, the effervescent micro-quartier that was once the preserve of grocers, African hair salons and authentic Indian diners that now share space with neo-bistros, natural wine bars and global street food outlets.

Metro: République, Château d'Eau, Jacques-Bonsergent, Colonial-Fabien, Goncourt, Gare de l'Est.

→ *The Canal Saint-Martin from the Passerelle Bichat*

SIGHTS
1. Galerie Miranda

SHOPPING
2. Macon & Lesquoy
3. Henriette H

EATING
4. Déviant
5. Le Verre Volé
6. Miznon

EATING & DRINKING
7. Ten Belles
8. Le Comptoir Général

DRINKING
9. Le Syndicat
10. La Java

1 GALERIE MIRANDA

21 rue du Château d'Eau,
75010
01 40 38 36 53
www.galeriemiranda.com
Open Tues–Fri 12pm–7pm,
Sat 10am–6pm
Metro République, Jacques
Bonsergent
[MAP p. 178 C3]

This light-drenched little shopfront gallery is a stylish space, fitted out simply in pine and with custom Socialite Family chairs. Exhibitions feature photographic artists who are established in their own regions but relatively new to European eyes, as well as lesser-known bodies of work from international stars. Past shows have featured American avant-guardists Jo Ann Callis and Nancy Wilson-Pajic; both with work that's startlingly prescient but vastly different from each other. Gallery director Miranda Salt is a Franco–Australian photography curator and art advisor who once worked in bookselling and publishing, and here she brings together both passions, with a beautiful collection of photographic books and related titles to browse and buy. New books are chosen to accompany each exhibition, and cover the life and work of the photographers, as well as related works by other artists, writers and critics.

POCKET TIP
A bonus for photophiles: the site of the diorama and laboratory of photography pioneer Louis Daguerre is just around the corner.

2 MACON & LESQUOY

37 rue Yves Toudic, 75010
09 53 92 89 70
www.maconetlesquoy.com
Open Mon 2.30–7.30pm,
Tues–Thurs 11.30am–2pm &
3–7.30pm, Fri–Sat 11.30am–
7.30pm
Metro République, Jacques
Bonsergent
[MAP p. 178 C2]

POCKET TIP
Coffee time? Brunch kings
Holybelly (rue Lucien
Sampaix), Blackburn (rue
de Faubourg Saint-Martin)
and Le 52 (Faubourg
Saint-Denis) won't
disappoint.

Inspired by the elegance and
precision of military badges,
Anne-Laure Lesquoy and
Marie Macon have whipped up
a huge international following
for their bold, beautifully
crafted brooches that defy
all conventions (even brooch
naysayers will go for these).
Each is hand-embroidered in
Portugal, with fine metallic
thread on felt, using a
traditional technique: the
designers see their mission
as one of democratising
something usually reserved
for luxury fashion. Motifs
roam from political slogans
to vegetables to anatomically
correct hearts to clouds to
teardrops to kitchen knives.
All are as delightfully rendered
as they are slyly humourous.
This, the designers' first
shopfront, stocks each seasonal
range; you can gleefully mix
and match pieces to tell your
own story. As well as the
pinnables, there are heat-
sealable patches, leather goods
and other accessories.

3 HENRIETTE H

24 rue du Chateau d'Eau,
75010
www.henrietteh.com
Open Tues–Fri 11am–6.30pm,
Sat 2–7pm
Metro: République, Jacques
Bonsergent
[MAP p. 178 C3]

Designer Sarah Stagliano's
lingerie and basics lines are
made only from the finest
white cotton voile and jersey,
with perhaps a lace insert
here and there. Lined up in
the pretty space are shirts,
boxers and tees for men,
ruched knickers, camisoles
and triangle bras for women.
All have an elegant purity and
a French ingénue sexiness;
the sole embellishment an
embroidered name, bon
mot or double entendre,
from 'oh oui' to 'enlève moi'
and 'amoureuse'. Can't
choose? Special requests?
Your partner's name in pink,
red or blue? Yes, you can
have anything you desire
embroidered and, yes, anything
goes – Parisians are hard to
shock and confidentiality is
guaranteed. Henriette H's first
candle, the Allemeuse (tease),
is made in France's perfume
capital Grasse and is a potent,
voluptuous mix of boudoir-
friendly orange, ginger, ylang-
ylang, myrrh and benzoin.
Gift boxes of knickers for two
cater to both hetero and same
sex couples.

POCKET TIP
Ask to see the salle de mariage of the 10th's Mairie (town hall) to see the startling La Fraternité, by sculptor (and exiled Communard) Jules Dalou.

4 DÉVIANT

39 rue des Petites Écuries,
75010
01 48 24 66 79
www.vivantparis.com
Open Tues–Sat 6.30pm–1am
Metro Poissonnière
[MAP p. 178 A2]

You could of course just pull
up at this austere marble-clad
shopfront for a glass of pet-nat
or a natural Sicilian. But then,
why would you want to miss
out on the very fine small plates
that are being prepared before
your eyes? Owned by some
of the 10th's culinary shakers
and movers, Arnaud Lacombe
and Pierre Touitou, you'll soon
discover that eating on your
feet, elbow-to-elbow has never
felt so good. A warm salad
arrives of zucchinis teamed
with fresh almonds and sour
cherries and could be followed
by a sliced steak baton on a
bed of mustard and strewn
with mint. Less delicate but
so more-more-moreish, there's
chicken wings in a volatile
marinade or a totally Tunisian,
utterly lip-licking brik, a runny
egg and tuna pastry served on
brown paper straight from the
fryer with a dab of housemade
harissa. Wines, because of
their small producer origins, hit
a level a little above usual wine
bar prices, but it's a good place
to get to know who's who in
the natural wine world.

POCKET TIP
From Faubourg
Saint-Denis look for
the poetically named
embrace of streets: rue
de la Fidélité, Passage
du Désir, rue de Paradis,
and rue Bleue.

5 LE VERRE VOLÉ

67 rue de Lancry, 75010
01 48 03 17 34
www.leverrevole.fr
Open daily 12.30pm–2.30pm
& 7.30–10pm
Metro: République, Jacques
Bonsergent
[MAP p. 178 C2]

This tiny wine bar and bistro
became well known on the
global foodie grapevine over
a decade ago. While the
fabled crowds have thinned
a tad (yes, you can now
occasionally nab an early
table for lunch or dinner
without booking), their food
and wine goes from strength
to strength. Don't come here
for stylist-ordained decor: the
wine-clad walls and battered
chairs and tables are entirely
utilitarian, if unexpectedly
romantic. Instead you'll get
cult natural wines (they're one
of the Paris pioneers of the
movement) served without a
hint of pretension, and small
and large plate dining that's
also gimmick free but full of
best-quality seasonal produce,
skillful saucing and pretty
plating. Order a 'traditional
plats' – say the boudin noir
maison (house black pudding)
with puree or pick and choose
from mostly seafood starters,
say sublime 'live-kill' shrimps
pan-fried in the Bordier
butter, or marinated trout
with samphire and spring
cabbage. Lunch deals are
exceptional value.

POCKET TIP

Pick up sandwiches and
a bottle for *en plein air*
lunches at Le Verre Volé's
epicerie and cave (rue de
la Folie-Méricourt), just
over in the 11th.

93

6 MIZNON

37 Quai de Valmy, 75010
Open Sun–Thurs 12pm–
11.30pm, Fri 12pm–3.30pm
Metro République, Jacques
Bonsergent
[MAP p. 179 D3]

Israeli superstar chef Eyal
Shani shook up Paris'
traditional falafel strip down in
the Pletzl (the Marais' Jewish
quartier) with his fresh take on
the stuffed pita, but his canal-
side place, is on another scale
altogether. Here, there's both
inside and terrace seating, a
frenetic open kitchen, a loud
rock and roll soundtrack and
daily queues. There's also,
perversely, almost everything
but falafel, but the crowds of
young locals packing out this
place obviously don't mind.
Beef Bourguignon in a pita
begs the question: why has
no one thought of this before?
Then there's ratatouille or
minute steak and egg fillings
that, while also as French as
can be, are given a Levantine
makeover and strewn with
plenty of herbs, chopped salad
and other fresh flourishes. Or
try Shani's signature whole
baked cauliflower – delicious
as its many charred, splayed
versions look like on social
media, though how to actually
eat it eludes many. Too busy to
sit? Take away and team with
a bottle of Monoprix Rosé for a
perfect canal picnic.

7 TEN BELLE*S*

10 rue de la Grange aux Belles,
75010
01 42 40 90 78
www.tenbelles.com
Open Mon–Fri 8am–6pm,
Sat–Sun 9am–7pm
Metro Jacques Bonsergent
[MAP p. 178 C2]

When Ten Belles opened back
in 2010, good coffee was a
rare thing indeed in Paris. The
siren-song of a perfectly made
flat white helped transform
the picturesque little rue de
la Grange-aux-Belles into a
fashionable enclave and the
bijoux cafe is now flanked by
a florist, an organic produce
store and makers' ateliers.
An international barista
army still serves up expertly
made espresso and filter with
beans from owners Anselme
Blayney and Thomas Lehoux's
Brûlerie Belleville, along with a
changing rota of guest roasters
(say Copenhagen's April or
London's Assembly). The food
menu is Anglo-inflected care of
their sibling Ten Belles Bakery
in the 11th. The sausage
rolls are legendary, there's
weekend croque monsieurs
and weekday salads and
overstuffed sandwiches.
Cookies, scones and brownies
join French favourites like
financiers and slabs of a
delicious lemon *quart a quart*
(pound) cake.

POCKET TIP
Anna Trattles and Alice
Quillet bake divine
sourdough breads and
savoury pies at Ten
Belles Bread (17–19 rue
Breguet) in the 11th's
Roquette quartier.

8 LE COMPTOIR GÉNÉRAL

80 Quai de Jemmapes, 75010
01 44 88 24 48
www.lecomptoirgeneral.com
Open daily 11am–2am
Metro Jacques Bonsergent,
Goncourt
[MAP p. 179 D2]

A sprawling cool kids' theme park of some 600 square metres, come for a Franco–African weekend brunch or late afternoon rum and ginger, but stay for a wander through the ramble of vintage furnished rooms or linger in the lush courtyard garden. That's if you can find the unmarked entrance (you will, then just keep going down the lane). This non-profit's mission statement says it all: 'whomever you may be, this hideaway, this temple of ghetto culture, shall be open to you every day of the week ...'. A recent addition of the bow of a sailing ship now houses the bar and the decor continues to evolve, making for surprises on repeat visits. The brunch remains huge though, with all-you-can-eat curries, quiches and fresh tropical juices, and the drinks list never disappoints, with super strong ti-punches and other rum-based fun times. Come early (and stay late) on the weekend for excellent world, reggae or Afro-funk DJs and an all embracing, all dancing, big drinking crowd.

9 LE /YNDICAT

51 rue du Faubourg Saint-
Denis, 75010
www.syndicatcocktailclub.com
Open Mon–Sat 6pm–2am
Metro Chateau d'Eau
[MAP p. 178 B2]

This grunge-luxe hip-hop
drenched drinking hole was
created by Sullivan Doh and
Romain Le Mouellic with the
express aim to Frenchify the
city's cocktails, and keep
prices down. Sparking a city-
wide trend (yes these guys
were the first), cocktails here
use Cognac and Armagnac –
spirits many associate with
their grandparents – along with
beautiful boutique French gins,
absinthe, eau de vies and some
obscure regional rarities. The
super creative list reads like
a poem, sometimes a risqué
ditty, with Saix en Provence –
Armagnac, watermelon syrup,
lemon and lavender foam –
setting the tone for the 'Insane
in Saint Denis Style' section.
But it's the 'classiques' that are
the charm, including a Brexit
appropriate 'gen tonique' done
with French Pontarlier gentian
liqueur and a herb-infused
house-made tonic water.
Snacks are as simple as the
gold lame entrance curtains are
glam: little pots of artichoke or
capsicum cream with a basket
of very good bread.

POCKET TIP
If you're wanting to
kick on after Faubourg
Saint-Denis drinks, the
dancefloor at Hôtel
Bourbon opens its
doors from midnight
to dawn.

LE SYNJICA

ORGANISATION DE DÉFEN
DES SPIRITUEUX FRANÇA

10 LA JAVA

105 rue du Faubourg du
Temple, 75010
01 42 02 20 52
www.la-java.fr
Open Thurs–Sat 11pm–6am
Metro Goncourt
[MAP p. 179 E2]

Over the canal and up the hill,
where it gets suddenly grungy
and feels like Belleville despite
the official arrondissement
demarcation, the stage of
this little 1920s' basement
concert hall was once graced
by Piaf and Django Reinheart.
A den of vice in the '70s,
salsa haunt in the '80s, it then
became a favoured dansant
(ballroom dancing) haunt in
the '90s. Though, nostalgic
it ain't. Oxblood vinyl booths
and faded murals of a Paris
long gone surround what is
now a late night dance floor
for techno, electronic, dub,
house, ambient and world DJs
as well as live acts. La Java's
program is broad, so time your
visit (the website has a reliably
up-to-date calendar). Once
that's sorted here's the deal:
drinks come in plastic cups,
are of questionable quality
and you might be shouted at
if you ask for a glass of water.
Oh and the toilet is unisex and
lit as if for an interrogation.
But the crowds are friendly,
good looking and here to
dance, the door policy next
to non-existent, and it's open
until dawn.

BASTILLE, OBERKAMPF & ALIGRE, 11TH & 12TH

There's but a few stones left of the actual Bastille, where the French Revolution really got going, but the Colonne de Juillet topped roundabout on its site is still the favoured setting for any form of Parisian protest (which, this being France, is always on the cards). It's Génie de la Liberté (spirit of freedom) figure (not, in fact, cupid) is also one of your best bets for visual navigation. The surrounding streets of Bastille were once the preserve of small furniture factories and artisans' workshops, most of which survived beyond the boulevards, making for a refreshingly low-rise precinct. Its (once) cheaper rents drew bohemian residents from the '80s onwards.

Overkampf sees most of the late-night action now, but there's still plenty of drinking options to explore in the streets around rue Charonne. Meanwhile, the dining scene has never been more vibrant, with some of the city's most exciting young chefs hanging their shingle here. Shopping is similarly switched on, with rue Charonne's French midrange labels mixing it up with lots of independent makers, a slew of vinyl shops and vintage furniture dealers. Across the chain-store lined rue du Faubourg Saint-Antoine, the 12th's less-touristed streets are home to the Marché d'Aligre (*see* p. 106) and more great laid-back dining and drinking.

Metro: Bastille, Ledru-Rollin, Gare du Lyon, rue Saint-Maur, Oberkampf, Père Lachaise

→ *Café Méricourt on the rue de la Folie Méricourt*

1 COULÉE VERTE

1 Coulée verte René-Dumont,
75012
Open daily 7.30am–8.30pm
Metro Bastille, Gare du Lyon
[MAP p. 188 A4]

This lush green corridor, officially the Coulée verte René-Dumont, but also known as the Promendade Plantée, was the world's first elevated park, crafted from a long abandoned railway line and somewhat ignored by everyone until only recently. This 4.5-kilometre route is far from a simple walking track: rather it's an ambulatory adventure among roses, lavender, wisteria, vines, shrubs, hazelnut trees and bamboo thickets, in parts hovering 10-metres above ground. Beginning at the **Viaduc des Artes**, historic vaults with a strip of underwhelming shops, stairs or a lift take you to its first, pedestrian-only section. It's here you'll get stunning rooftop views, including the enormous beefy atlantes (male carytids) that line the fabulously post-modern Police commissariat building, the path then winds between (and, in one case, through) typical Parisian buildings. The old Vincennes railway viaduct drops back to street level at the **Jardin de Reuilly** (from where you can cycle), and continues on to the park **Bois de Vincennes**.

2 FRENCH TROTTER/

30 rue de Charonne, 75011
01 47 00 84 35
www.frenchtrotters.fr
Open Mon 1.30–7.30pm,
Tues–Sat 11.30am–7.30pm
Metro Ledru Rollin
[MAP p. 188 B3]

Time poor and on a one-hit shopping mission? There's a small well-curated selection of homewares, jewellery and accessories, as well as magazines and beautiful candles, to discover here, along with a savvy collection of mens' and womens' clothing and accessories. Owners Carole and Clarent Dehlouz design the house labels respectively; both lines feauturing pieces that might carry over from season to season with just fabrics and prints, buttons or trims updated. It's an addictive model that wins life-long label converts. This bijou super store also packs in an inspiring collection of other low-key designers, including clever picks from everyone's favourite Frenchies A.P.C and Le Mont Saint Michel alongside Italian luxury shirtmakers Forte_Forte and sublimely detailed ankle boots and disco-ready sandals from Michel Vivien. Cross label collaborations happen too, with the duo recently pairing with French shoemakers Anthropologie and scarf company Moismont.

POCKET TIP

For 20th-century design, pore over the work of Jean Prouvé, Charlotte Perriand, Pierre Jeanneret and Le Corbusier furniture at the 11th's Galerie Patrick Seguin (5 rue des Taillandjers).

103

3 LE BAIGNEUR

5 rue de la Folie Méricourt,
75011
09 86 09 32 58
www.lebaigneur.fr
Open Tues–Sat 11am–8pm
Metro Saint-Ambroise
[MAP p. 188 A1]

A genuinely made-in-Paris
product, these wonderful
artisan soaps, oils and lotions
are made right here in the
open workshop. An artful mix
of industrial chic and stylish
bathroom decor, the geometric
green, navy and white look
is about as far from twee as a
soap shop can get. Baigneur's
young creators are dedicated
to the traditional technique
of cold saponification, which
unlike commercial techniques
retains natural glycerines,
protecting the hydrolipidic
film of your skin. Must-have
take homes beyond the
beautifully toned soap blocks
are the facial oils, a French
speciality, infused with hemp
or clove, or with exfoliating
coconut pulp, and can be used
post-shaving or as a cleanser
or moisturiser, too. While the
range is essentially unisex, the
porcelain shaving bowls with a
calendula, St. John's Wort and
oat extract beard soap and Jura
beech badger shaving brush
will make perfect presents for
men. This is a plastic-free zone,
with zero packaging or strictly
recyclable glass and paper.

POCKET TIP

Vinyl is king in the
11th: kick off your crate
digging at Vinyl Office
(9 rue Trousseau) or
Le Silence de la Rue
(39 rue Faidherbe).

4 MARCHÉ D'ALIGRE

Place d'Aligre, 75012
01 45 11 71 11
www.marchedaligre.free.fr
Open Tues–Sun 9am–12.30pm
(outdoor stalls), Tues–Sat
4–7.30pm (Marché Beauvau)
Metro Ledru-Rollin
[MAP p. 188 B4]

Marché d'Aligre might not
offer postcard views or poshly
displayed produce but it is one
of the city's most vibrant and
varied neighbourhood markets,
offering fruit, vegetables
and flowers from a couple of
streets of outdoor stalls. It's
also one of the only one that
opens daily (with the exception
of Monday). At its centre, the
covered Marché Beauvau
offers more of the same, as
well as game, charcuterie,
cheese and seafood counters.
On the curving sweep of
the Place d'Aligre there's a
daily flea market, with stalls
specialising in second-hand
designer clothes, ceramics,
paintings, traditional masks
and sculptures from the Cote
d'Ivoire, CDs and well, just
great old French junk. Canny
locals have been known to
pick up pristine YSL suits here
for next to nix, and if you're
patient and have the knack,
the miles of books and vinyl
can yield some very tasty
finds indeed.

POCKET TIP
Paris' best vide-greniers
(empty attic) – huge street
garage sales – are in
the 11th's rue Charonne
(mid May) and the 20th's
Village Jourdain (late
September).

5 BUFFET

8 rue de la Main d'Or, 75011
01 83 89 63 82
www.restaurantbuffet.fr
Open Tues–Sat 12.30pm–
2.30pm & 7–11pm
Metro Ledru-Rollin
[MAP p. 188 B4]

First things first: there's no
buffet. The name refers to the
owner, the one Jean-Charles
Buffet. If restaurant lineage
matters to you, he's been
behind several of the 11th's
most successful kitchens,
including the perennially
packed Au Passage. This place
looks little different from the
old bar it took over a couple
of years back, with red-and-
white-check tablecloths
topping a couple of rooms of
dark wood bistro furniture.
The menu is smart and simple,
though the food on the plate
is more sophisticated than
first impressions may suggest.
Your steak and bone marrow
or sausage and lentils will
have interesting garnishes,
perhaps charry leeks or a little
herb salad, your dessert, that
strawberry soup, will come
with a dollop of vanilla bean-
flecked crème fraiche. Wines
are all organic too. There's a
good-value lunch formula, and
if you come early you're all
but guaranteed a table. Plus
Buffet's resistance to googling
means you'll more likely be on
the prized Moleskin banquette
with local creatives, rather
than tourists.

POCKET TIP

Rue Amelot's length is
dotted with restaurants, from
small plates and natural
wine veterans Le Clown
Bar to Uzbekistani and
Vietnamese cheapies.

6 YARD

6 rue de Mont-Louis, 75011
01 40 09 70 30
www.yard-restaurant.com
Open Mon–Fri 12pm–2.30pm
& 8–10.30pm
Metro Philippe Auguste
[MAP p. 188 C2]

In the vibrant but locals-focused north-eastern reaches of the 11th, Yard has long been a firm favourite of the Parisian neo-bistro scene despite a recent sabbatical. With an appealing monochrome makeover, they're back with food that's as fresh and appealing as ever, great lunch deals and a menu that effortlessly roams across European borders here or contentedly stays in France. A charcoal-toned industrial exterior hides a pretty dining room, cosy in winter when you can have ravioli with fromage frais and chanterelle mushrooms or veal chops sliced right from the bone, or airy and open to the street in summer, where there'll be watercress soup with a poached egg, plaice with bitter orange-scented butter and tarragon, then a quivery, rose-scented pannacotta with rhubarb. Wine runs to the edgier side of natural with some wonderful small producer bottles on offer. If it's warm you can eat outside on the quiet street; they also have a bar next door.

POCKET TIP

For gluten-free sourdough loaves, focaccia and an enticing range of cakes, tarts and biscuits, head to boulangerie-cafe Chambelland (14 rue Ternaux, 11th).

7 SEPTIME LA CAVE

3 rue Basfroi, 75011
01 43 67 14 87
www.septime-charonne.fr
Open daily 4–11pm (bar),
Tues–Fri 12.15pm–2pm
& Mon–Fri 7.30–10pm
(restaurant)
Metro Ledru-Rollin, Charonne
[MAP p. 188 B3]

Septime's rustic cellar bar is atmospheric and easy-to-love, an excellent addition to the perennially popular Septime restaurant family (they also run seafood hotspot Clamato). Although you can only eat snacks here, and you'll be sitting on stools, if not crates, these are predictably tasty dishes that use fabulous produce and are plated to please the eye. Fat anchovies are scattered with crunchy buckwheat and draped across freshly made ricotta, there's sliced Bellotta ham sprinkled with toasty smashed hazelnuts or marinated artichokes and green onions, and the accompanying bread basket might just feature one of the city's best sourdough. The wine list is surprising and inspiring, drawn from across Europe, with pét-nats and special sulphite-frees, in the all-natural list. And yes, it's a wine shop too so you can take away, with the wine-smart staff always ready to help you choose.

8 CAFÉ MÉRICOURT

22 rue de la Folie Méricourt,
75011
01 58 30 98 02
www.cafemericourt.com
Open daily 9am–6pm
(kitchen until 3pm)
Metro Saint-Ambroise
[MAP p. 188 A1]

This bright cafe with its
Scandi-vibing interior was one
of the pioneers of the Folie-
Méricourt's reinvention. Let's
call it a shakshuka-driven
boom, with locals, expats
and visitors all clamouring for
the cafe's signature Tunisian
brunch dish: a moreish mix
of eggs baked into tomato,
capsicum and harissa. Join the
flocks of freelancers as they
gather first thing for meetings
over house-made bircher
with cottage cheese and fried
almonds or fleur d'orange
scented ricotta pancakes. If
you're in need of respite from
Parisian over-indulgence,
the lunch bowls of quinoa,
avocado, greens and pickles
are clean-eating heaven.
Friendly staff will also whip
you up a good flat white made
with their locally roasted house
blend beans and there's plenty
of people watching, magazines
and bar chat to while away a
few hours.

POCKET TIP
The 11th's snaking, atmospheric Folie-Méricourt strip is blooming, with drinking spots, low-key restaurants and new independent shops aplenty.

9 LE BARON ROUGE

1 rue Théophile Roussel, 75012
01 43 43 14 32
Open Mon 5–10pm, Tues–Fri
10am–2pm & 5–10pm, Sat
10am–10pm, Sun 10am–4pm
Metro Ledru-Rollin
[MAP p. 188 B4]

Le Baron Rouge manages to
tread the tightrope of being
a defiantly local Parisian
bar while at the same time
fulfilling almost everyone's
fantasy of one. Visitors come
for a peek, and many end
up staying, but the good,
and very affordable, French
whites, reds and sparklings
keep flowing regardless.
The tunes, care of a crew
of moonlighting musician/
composer/artist bartenders,
are never dull, never generic,
and the eccentric bonhomie
is, one hopes, eternal. Yes,
this is somewhere that it's
perfectly acceptable to quaff a
Saturday morning Muscadet at
the zinc bar post market shop,
and absolutely no problem if
you're still here with your new
friends at closing, you won't
be the only one (last drinks
do, mercifully, come early, at
10pm). Stomach liners include
freshly shucked oysters on
Sundays from October to April,
and generous everyday platters
of well-chosen charcuterie,
fish rillettes and cheese year
round. Tip a little on your first
drink and you may find all your
future glasses runneth over.

POCKET TIP
Book ahead for local's
favourite l'Ébauchoir
(43 rue de Cîteaux, 12th),
although a dinner of
hearty share plates can
also be had at Siffleur de
Ballons, their wine bar
across the road.

10 L'INTERNATIONAL

5/7 rue Moret, 75011
09 50 57 60 50
www.linternational.fr
Open Tues–Thurs 7pm–1am,
Fri–Sat 7pm–6am
Metro Ménilmontant,
Parmentier
[MAP p. 179 F3]

Although Parisians complain their nightlife's no longer up to that of Berlin or Antwerp or Oslo, the city's live music scene has remained pretty formidable. International acts play the big concert halls most nights but Paris also does mid-size venues really well. Most of these can be found either in Pigalle and Montmarte or here in Oberkampf and up the hill into Ménilmontant. L'International is a decade-old stayer and is a nicely hassle-free place to see a band or DJ, with mostly local, often great, talent every night. Upstairs there's a rowdy, cavernous, vintage-furniture stacked bar, downstairs you'll find your standard dank, low-ceilinged basement band room. Nightly free acts might be of the guitar-led persuasion but there's also folk, electro and hip-hop on the calendar. No one really turns up here until late, but if you're not fussed keeping the bar staff company, there's a two-hour happy hour from 7pm.

MONTMARTRE, CHÂTEAU ROUGE & BARBÈS, 18TH

Montmarte's network of ancient cobbled streets, hidden staircases and breathtakingly vertiginous vistas make it one of Paris' most fascinating and photogenic destinations. Artists of all persuasions, including Pablo Picasso, Eric Satie and Gertrude Stein, were lured here by its cheap rents and flourishing dancehalls at the end of the 19th-century. Monmartre old-timers Moulin Rouge and Au Lapin Agile – both are over a century old – still dish out the four Bs (bubbly, boas, boobs and bums) on a nightly basis. Place du Tertre and its 'artists' has become a tacky sideshow, but much of the 18th has managed to retain a charming, villagey feel. There's many a low-key place to perch with a drink and watch the sunset, little squares and endless stairs to explore and even a postage-stamp sized working vineyard, the Clos Montmartre, to discover. Head east of the 'Butte' – Sacré-Coeur's hill (see p. 116) – and you'll also be in one of Paris' most culturally diverse neighbourhoods, with large west and north African communities in Château Rouge, Barbès and Goutte d'Or, and fabulous produce markets, cheap eats, as well as a growing number of hipster hangouts.

Metro: Abbesses, Anvers, Barbès-Rochechouart, Château Rouge, Lamarck-Caulaincourt

→ *Café Tabac from the rue Ravignan*

RUE DURANTIN

1 SACRÉ-COEUR

35 rue du Chevalier de la Barre,
75018
01 53 41 89 00
www.sacre-coeur-montmartre.com
Open daily 6am–10.30pm
Metro Anvers, Château Rouge
[MAP p. 173 D2]

The five white domes of this
basilica can be seen from
nearly every corner of Paris,
sitting atop the city's highest
point, and lit from below at
night, they can seem as if a
ghostly presence. Like the
Eiffel Tower and Notre-Dame,
there's no avoiding the crowds.
Still, a metro ticket will get you
up the funicular (all 108 metres)
and once at the top, the views
from the broad parvis and
the dome, some 300 steps
further up, are breathtaking.
Inside, the late 19th-century
bombast, marble expanses and
a supersized Jesus mosaic runs
to kitsch, but when candles are
lit and the grand organ plays at
Sunday mass (11am, 6pm and
10pm) or vespers (4pm), it can
be very affecting, even for the
less than devout. Sacré-Coeur's
spectacular siting in 1875 was
not incidental (nor just for
the views). It commemorates
a return to pro-monarchist
piety after the fall of the Paris
Commune in 1871; Montmartre
was where this final of Paris'
19th-century revolutionary
movements kicked off.

POCKET TIP
Use passage Cottin
(Château Rouge metro) to
escape the Sacré-Coeur-
bound throng (also grab
a coffee at rue Lamarck's
Hardware Société
on the way).

2 MAISON CHÂTEAU ROUGE

40 rue Myrha, 75018
www.maison-chateaurouge.com
Open Mon 2–7pm & Tues–Sat
11am–7pm
Metro Château Rouge,
Barbès–Rochechouart
[MAP p. 173 F2]

Tucked between rue Myrha's traditional West African wax cloth shops and grocers, this yellow-and-white-striped shopfront is more social hub than rarefied retail environment. Born out of a not-for-profit enterprise founded by Youssouf and Mamadou Fofana, along with Mehdi Bathily and Yoann Maillé, it celebrates the brothers' Franco–African heritage and aims to bring their culture to the world. Ranges are designed right here, traditional textiles are sourced from importer neighbours or artisans in Senegal while their mens- and womenswear are made in Paris or West Africa. The bombers, shirts, pants, skirts and tees draw on preppy sportswear, a beautiful contrast with the exuberant illustration and colours of wax cloth. New projects are always in the works, whether that's a house bissap (hibiscus flower) juice or big-name collaborations; there's accessories, jewellery and magazines to browse too.

POCKET TIP

Marché aux Puces de Saint-Ouen, also known as Clignancourt, or Les Puces, is Paris' largest flea market, a mini-city of vintage and antique dealers, open Saturday to Monday.

3 L'OBJET QUI PARLE

86 rue des Martyrs, 75018
objetquiparle.fr
Open Mon–Sat 1.30–7.30pm
Metro Abbesses, Pigalle
[MAP p. 173 D3]

No time to trawl Marché aux Puces de Saint-Oeun? Head to this hole-in-the-wall favourite of Parisian art directors and set designers, where a veteran collector with a superbly idiosyncratic eye has already done the hard yards for you. The pieces here murmur, sing and sometimes shout their intriguing back stories: naïve portraits of infantrymen daubed on the Belgian front and 1920s' vaudeville masks the size of lampshades hover over cabinets of religious artefacts and fittings from long-demolished hotels. Outside, a box full of elegant wax hands await new homes, while within a taxidermy heron and Madonna peer from a high perch. If your decorating tastes tend more to *Côté Sud* magazine than Dada dreamscape, there's a large stock of well-priced, easily-packed porcelain, glassware and linen, including beautiful bowls for your morning café au lait or chocolat chaud (hot chocolate).

POCKET TIP
Try the fleamarkets at Montreuil (20th), Porte de Vanves (14th) or Marché d'Aligre (see p. 106).

l'Objet qui Parle

4 A.P.C. SURPLUS

20 rue André del Sarte, 75018
01 42 62 10 88
www.apc.fr
Open Mon–Sat 12pm–7.30pm
Metro Château Rouge,
Barbès Rochechouart
[MAP p. 173 E2]

Jean Touitou's A.P.C., the three-decades' old Parisian label that's come to define a certain brainy, pared-back French style, makes the kind of clothes where past seasons' stock can be the main draw rather than a short straw. Their boutiques now dot the capital (and many cities around the world) but this surplus outlet is still something of an open secret, rarely as crowded as you might imagine. Racks are arranged by colour, so have a flip through for the shirts, smocks, pantsuits and jackets that you'd fallen in love with but by fate or restraint never found their way into your wardrobe. Discounts hover between 40 and 60 per cent off. They also stock non-discounted key pieces, such as the house quilts from past run dress and shirt fabric, home fragrances and their cult jeans and shoes. Mens- and womens-wear shops sit side by side.

POCKET TIP

Below the Butte, Marché Saint-Pierre is one of Paris' historic mercantile zones, with whole streets of huge competing textile emporiums.

5 CORPUS CHRISTI

84 rue des Martyrs, 75018
01 42 57 77 77
www.corpuschristi.fr
Open Tues–Sat 11.30am–
7.30pm, Sun 1.30–7.30pm
Metro Abbesses, Pigalle
[MAP p. 173 D3]

Intriguing window displays
will pull you into this equally
intriguing shop, where
bracelets, rings, necklaces
and earrings for both men
and women hang from deer
horns or sit beneath specimen
domes. Designer Thierry
Gougenot, once a painter,
is inspired by Baroque
architecture, rock and roll,
sacred art and tribal decoration
and his work eschews trends.
Rather he draws on religious
iconography and there's a
delicate Gothic edge to his
crosses, articulated skeletons,
reliquaries, orbs, flowers and
feathers. Most of the pieces
are crafted with sterling silver,
22-carat gold vermeil, pearls
and semi-precious stone so
sit at a price point between
costume and fine jewellery –
perfect Parisian present-to-self
fodder. Though if you're after
more serious baubles, there's
a small pure gold and precious
jewel range that's even more
delicate and lovely.

MONTMARTRE, CHÂTEAU ROUGE
& BARBÉS, 18TH

6 LE BAL

6 Impasse de la Défense,
75018
www.le-bal.fr
01 44 70 75 51
Open Wed 12pm–10pm,
Thurs–Sun 12pm–7pm (gallery)
Wed–Sat 12pm–11pm, Sun
12pm–7pm (Café Otto)
Metro Place de Clichy
[MAP p. 172 B2]

Venture up past the hectic
Place de Clichy to this
hidden away gallery, cafe
and bookshop, a former
dance hall and sometime
bordello. Two spaces celebrate
contemporary image making
via photography, video, film
and new media. There's a
good mix of monographic
and curated group shows;
over the last decade they've
shown big-name international
photographers, such as
Antoine d'Agata and Paul
Graham. Also specialising in
contemporary photographic
work, the attached **bookshop**
stocks photobooks, non-
mainstream films, works
of theory and international
photography magazines. The
attached **Café Otto**, now with
Austrian chef Lisa Machian at
the helm, serves up a great mix
of alpine and eastern flavours
joining Viennese favourites like
schnitzel with all the trimmings
(lemon, buttered potatoes,
cherry jam) or frittaten soup, a
rich broth with sliced pancakes
in the place of noodles.

122

7 FICHON

98 rue Marcadet, 75018
09 70 94 52 14
www.fichon.fr
Open Tues–Sat 12.30pm–
2.30pm & 7.30–10.30pm
Metro Jules Joffrin
[MAP p. 173 E1]

Part seafood shack, part wine bar, there's a casual ease to Fichon, a corner shopfront that contrasts traditional raw sandstone walls with bright scale-like tiles in seaside shades. The super fresh aquatic produce and natural wines on offer are both given much respect. Dishes are built around raw, steamed or gently seared fish or seafood, techniques that bring subtle flavours and textures to the fore. Start with wild Normandy oysters and bulots (sea snails) and mayonnaise maison, then settle on a plate of smoked tuna charcuterie, a confit trout with passionfruit or a tataki of bonito with beets, grapefruit and black sesame. Owner Matthieu Dewilde's wine trade background means his list of organic and biodynamic wines is well considered, and all chosen to complement various fishy flavours. He'll find the right bottle for your order, perhaps a little acid, or mineral, or iodine; there's some very interesting drops to try, from France but also other less known European wine regions.

POCKET TIP
The bronze with the gleaming breasts on Montmartre's Place Dalida memorialises late French–Egyptian singer Dalida (the shine comes from years of adoring rubs).

8 CAFÉ TABAC

1 rue Ravignan, 75018
01 42 51 44 53
Open Mon 8.30am–2pm,
Tues–Fri 8.30am–6pm, Sat–
Sun 9am–6.30pm
Metro Abbesses, Pigalle
[MAP p. 172 C2]

Franco–Australian couple
Frédéric and Charlotte Monnier
have conjured up a little bit
of Melbourne's famed coffee
culture on a quintessentially
Montmartre corner. Bucking
the third-wave coffee craze,
Fred turns out perfect flat
whites and espressos using
Genovese beans and a veteran
Italian–Australian coffee
roaster. Charlotte's interior
of red Tolix stools, geometric
floor tiles and a stunning
mid-century chandelier is a
happy-making backdrop for all.
They have a steady stream of
regulars – freelancers popping
in for a chat and a pastel de
nata (Portuguese custard tart)
or Gontran Cherrier croissant
at the bar, parents feeding cute
kids tartines and jam, and a
crew of caffeine-addicted locals
who seem quite content to stay
all day. If you're hungry try
the scrambled eggs with ham,
salmon or goats cheese, or fill
up on stuffed rolls and lots of
sweet treats.

9 MADAME ARTHUR

75 bis rue des Martyrs, 75018
01 40 05 08 10
www.divandumonde.com
Open Wed–Sat 8pm–6am
Metro Pigalle, Abbesses
[MAP p. 173 D3]

Fancy a night of cabaret? Can't face the Moulin Rouge crowds or Crazy Horse prices? The first 'travesti' floorshow in Paris opened in this 19th-century concert hall in 1946, and the show goes on again, after a 2015 revival. Eat, drink and be enchanted by a rollicking night of French song – think canonical hits from Johnny Hallyday, Edith Piaf and Dalida – along with much dancing and humour. There's a delicious rawness to the performances and costumes that will transport you back to Montmartre's glory days, as does the eccentrically decorated space. There are two stages, and two shows, at 9pm and 11pm, and you can book for either 'standing room' or a seated dinner deal. After midnight, the piano and accordion gives way to DJ sets and disco. If you'd like to test your knowledge of French popular culture, there's a quiz, with prizes, at 11pm on Fridays and Saturdays.

10 LE TRÈS PARTICULIER

Hôtel Particulier Montmartre
Pavillon D, Passage de la
Sorcière, 75018
01 53 41 81 40
www.hotel-particulier-
montmartre.com/bar
Open Mon–Sun 6pm–2am
Metro Lamarck-Caulaincourt
[MAP p. 172 C2]

The Hôtel Particulier Montmartre is a small, upmarket hotel set in a late 18th-century Directoire-style mansion and possesses one of the largest – and lushest – hotel gardens in the city. Arriving at its bar feels unmistakeably Parisian but also like you're embarking on a mythical quest. Your Ithaca is guarded by tall, locked gates, vertiginous stairs and the mysterious witch's rock – so don't let Google fool you. Instead, look for a subtly marked doorbell at 23 avenue Junot, announce yourself and head up the passage. Once there, pull up a chair out the front in the garden if the sun's out, or otherwise make for the basement Le Très Particulier where cocktails, concocted with literary or cinematic references, and using the hotel's own herbs and honey, can be sipped amid lush tropical plants in its rather covert-feeling conservatory.

POCKET TIP
Le Très Particulier's DJ sets, Wednesday through Saturday from 9.30pm and from 7pm on Sundays, pull a très particulier crowd too.

POCKET TIP

The 17th's Batignolles, west of Montmartre, rarely draws tourists, but has a village square, duckpond, children's playground, artists' studios, great wine bars and an organic produce market.

BELLEVILLE, MÉNILMONTANT & VILLETTE, 19TH & 20TH

Paris' north-east corner has been partying hard since long before it became part of the city proper in 1860. It's easy to imagine hilly, green Belleville and the neighbouring village of Ménilmontant flush with rough-and-ready bars and guinguettes (rustic tavern dance halls), welcoming all for 'country pleasures', i.e. boozy mayhem. The last few decades of gentrification this century has made the 19th & 20th a favourite of young creatives and bobo families, but you'll also notice rapid change has been gently resisted, with a lifestyle that's still relatively affordable and thriving Chinese and North African communities. Bars and live venues can be found on late-night favourite, rue de Ménilmontant, which runs down to meet the 11th's Oberkampf, or opt for the more grown-up wine bars, cafes and restaurants of Belleville's rue Dénoyez, boulevard de Belleville and around Bagnolet's Mama Shelter hotel. Further north, Parc de la Villette houses a number of new cultural venues, including Jean Nouvel's stunning Philharmonie de Paris, live venue Le Zenith and the Villette's Cité des Sciences et de l'Industrie, the city's sprawling science and industry museum. The Canal de l'Ourcq and the Bassin du Villette banks have also recently been transformed, with parks, hotels, restaurants and bars all lining the waterfront (and where, in high summer, you'll find the Paris Plage, an artificial beach).

Metro: Belleville, Pyrénées, Gambetta, Botzaris, Buttes Chaumont, Jaurès, Ourcq

↦ *The Eiffel Tower from Parc de Belleville*

SIGHTS
1. Cimetière du Père Lachaise
2. Parc des Buttes-Chaumont

SHOPPING & EATING
3. Le 104

EATING
4. Au Boeuf Couronné
5. Le Grand Bain

EATING & DRINKING
6. Le Fontaine de Belleville

DRINKING
7. Le Commune Punch Club
8. Paname Brewing Company

1 CIMETIÈRE DU PÈRE LACHAI∫E

8 boulevard de Ménilmontant,
75020
www.paris.fr/cimetieres
01 55 25 82 10
Open Mon–Fri 8am–5.30pm,
Sat from 8.30am, Sun from 9am
Metro Philippe Auguste,
Père Lachaise
[MAP p. 189 D1]

Beloved of Goths, lovers, melancholics and (dead) celebrity spotters, this is not only Paris' largest cemetery, its 5000 trees make it the city's largest park. Winding streets, high walls and hilly topography pair with over two hundred years of funerary style: poetic 19th-century sculptures, bombastic Haussmanian mausoleums, modern abstractions and eerie curiosities. Headstones are a who's-who of French cultural and civic life, with writers Apollinaire, Balzac, Proust, Gertrude Stein and Colette buried here, plus more recently film director Claude Chabrol and mime Marcel Marceau. Not to be missed, in the far north-east corner, is the Mur des Fédérés, marking the mass grave of 147 Communards, buried where they were shot in 1871. The most thronged of graves remain the expats – Jim Morrison's grunge site, and Jacob Epstein's sad tomb for Oscar Wilde.

2 PARC DES BUTTES-CHAUMONT

74 rue Botzaris, 75019
Open daily 7am–9pm
Metro Buttes Chaumont,
Botzaris
[MAP p. 185 B3]

For bucolic, rambling green spaces and spectacular city vistas, you can't really go past Buttes-Chaumont. Set in a former quarry, its unusual topography makes a simple walk in the park a grand adventure, with hills, knolls, ponds, cliffs and caves to explore, all watched over by its towering 1860s folly, the **Temple de la Sibylle**. If you've no time or inclination to sort a picnic, Buttes-Chaumont is blessed with a number of Belle Époque guinguettes (rustic taverns), all dating to 1861, including the sprawling pizza and party zone **Pavillon Puebla**, the upmarket if easy going **Pavillon du Lac** restaurant and terrace and the ebullient, eccentric **Rosa Bonheur**, named for the 19th-century landscape painter (whose name serendipitously means happiness). The latter serves up organic daytime plates and take-aways (instant picnic!), morphing into a LGBTIQ favourite at night and for boozy, loud Sunday afternoon sessions.

POCKET TIP

Villette's Cité des Sciences et de l'Industrie (30 avenue Corentin-Cariou), the largest science museum in Europe, has vast greenhouses, a planetarium and a 'city of children' space.

POCKET TIP

Belleville's arts
community holds an open
studio weekend in late
May; head to its most
noteworthy contemporary
space, Galerie Sultana
(10 rue Ramponeau)
year round.

3 LE 104

5 rue Curial, 75019
01 53 35 50 01
www.104.fr
Open Tues–Fri 12pm–7pm
(later for events), Sat–Sun from
11am–7pm
Metro Riquet
[MAP p. 186 A2]

The vast Centquatre ('cent-
cat') art centre (set in what
was once the City of Paris'
undertakers), is a vibrant
outpost in this slow-to-gentrify
Eastern neighbourhood. There
is a full calendar of live acts
across all music and dance
genres at night, while during
the day, you can join local
families relaxing in deckchairs
and watching roving acrobats
or dancers. Those with
under-fives are welcomed into
Maison des Petits, where
designer Matali Crasset's
signature poppy colours and
organic forms are a backdrop
of all sorts of all-weather play.
Pop-up shops from ethical
producers join a permanent
charity shop, **Emmaüs Défi**.
Café-Caché feeds and waters
104's audience, doubles as
the resident artists' canteen
and is also a local's favourite.
For night-time dining there's
the light loft space of **Grand
Central**, open until midnight
for French comfort food and
artisan beers and cider.

4 AU BOEUF COURONNÉ

188 avenue Jean Jaurès, 75019
01 42 39 44 44
www.boeuf-couronne.com
Open daily 12pm–3pm &
6.30pm–12am
Metro Porte de Pantin
[MAP p. 187 E3]

Opened in 1865, this steakhouse dates back to when Villette was the site of the city's slaughterhouse and meat market, and is still a place for multi-generational family meals. The long list of beef cuts, from 300g to a shareable 1.2kg, are all from Normandy and aged for at least 20 days. Tartare is a speciality and there's a very well-priced onglet (hanger steak) or 'butcher's choice' in (slightly) smaller portions. Sweets stay trad too: rum baba or flambéed crêpes Suzette. Designer Fabrice Ausset's recent fit-out, with tree-like brass lighting, geometric gold mirrors and miles of plump saignant-toned velvet, is a startling '70s homage. Meanwhile, staff seem as if from an Emile Zola novel: a primly suited maître d', the stern but kind matron taking your order, and clusters of coy servers. You'll be gunning for frites or purée, but order your Châteaubriand or entrecôte with the pommes soufflé, twice-fried potato slices that magically puff up into airy pillows – fabulous.

POCKET TIP

The contemporary organic design of the Philharmonie de Paris' 2400 seat concert hall (221 avenue Jean-Jaurès, 19th) makes for intimate and immersive performances.

5 LE GRAND BAIN

14 rue Dénoyez, 75020
09 83 02 72 02
www.legrandbainparis.com
Open daily 7–11.30pm
Metro Belleville
[MAP p. 179 F2]

Le Grand Bain wasn't the first
gourmet incursion into the
colourful grit of rue Dénoyez.
But with their arrival, this
heavily tagged, pedestrianised
strip, once the preserve of
corner bars and Maghrebi
take-aways, has become
Belleville's most vibrant eating
zone. Edward Delling-Williams
is on the pans and despite his
stellar pedigree (he helped put
Au Passage in the 11th on the
global foodie map), dishes read
simply and concisely on the
menu. What emerges from the
busy open kitchen is often also
pared back to essentials; join
the good-looking hordes for his
famous whole shoulder of lamb
or a braised bunny. Or instead
pick and choose from the small
plates, say kingfish crudo
pimped up with pork skin, or
grilled scallops with shiso in
dashi. Pair each with a glass of
the wine list's natural beauties,
including a few cracking pét-
nats. There's a confidence and
swagger to it all, but the space,
with its natural wood tables
and rustic exposed beams
is unflashy, welcoming and
warm, as are the staff.

POCKET TIP
Across the street at no. 7,
Delling-Williams' Le Petit
Grain bakes brilliant breads
and croissants using freshly
milled organic flour and
natural leavenings.

Reste : 1# x Lapin ± Salsify 11€

0x Pigeon → Lapin cote

1x Epaule

8 x Jalapenos 2

* ORMEAU, ENDIVE, MIRIN . 7€
* THON, RADIS, MAYONAISE . 7€
* CABILLAUD, CHOUFLEUR, PAPRIKA . 7€
* COUTEAUX, SALSA VERDE . 6€
* SEICHE, ENCRE . 7€
* TRUITE ENTIERE . 16€

* JALAPENOS, SPICY MAYO . 6€
* ASPERGE, HOLLANDAISE . 9€
* CELERI RAVE, ANCHOIS . 6€
* RUTABAGA, OEUFS DE HARENG . 6€
* TOPINAMBOURG, YAOURT . 5€
* SALADE DE CHOU de BXL, DULSE . 5€

6 LE FONTAINE DE BELLEVILLE

31–33 rue Juliette Dodu, 75010
09 81 75 54 54
www.cafesbelleville.com
Open daily 8am–10pm
Metro Colonel Fabien
[MAP p. 179 D1]

A reimagined neighbourly all-rounder that's been doing business since 1915, you can come for coffee and boiled eggs first thing, have a ham baguette for lunch or kick on until last call at 10pm. About that coffee: the Belleville Brûlerie, one of Paris' best roasteries, is a partner here, so it's excellent. The beautiful corner space has original painted mirrors, moulded high-ceilings and towering vases of flowers, making for a dreamy timelessness. Cakes are all housemade (the pain d'épice goes particularly well with a Valrhona hot chocolate on chilly afternoons) and in the evening there's beautiful cheeses, charcuterie, rillettes and pâté (the latter two Belleville-sourced). There are three whites, three reds by the glass, all natural plus a couple of Parisian craft beers to sample. Weekends are huge: on Saturdays there's free jazz from 4.30pm and on Sunday a brunch menu packs them in from 11am. Note that while it's officially in the 10th, Belleville is just across the road.

7 LE COMMUNE PUNCH CLUB

80 boulevard de Belleville,
75020
01 42 55 57 61
www.syndicatcocktailclub.com
Open Tues–Sat 11.30am–2am
(drinks from 6pm)
Metro Couronnes, Belleville
[MAP p. 179 F3]

POCKET TIP

For garage and grunge bands or day-long techno and underground electronic sets, head to La Station–Gare des Mines, just over the Périphérique (ring road).

With a deep enclosed terrace on a busy stretch of boulevard, you might not at first notice just how gorgeous this shopfront bar in fact is. When it's warm the party scene out front might feel like the place to be but one of the geometric brass and velvet stools at its punch bowl-lined bar is better for banter. Like parent bar Le Syndicat (*see* p. 98) in the 10th, all the spirits, aperitifs and wines here are French, though the drinks list also pays homage to Belleville's multicultural mix. Pineapple and bissap (hibiscus) juices, say, and lemongrass, cinnamon and coriander notes star in cocktails; absinthe is scented with tonka, pastis comes with a chilli kick. Spritzes eschew even the Italians, instead using a peppy Cap Corse aperitif. The soundtrack is mellow with reggae and dub early on, then veers into hip-hop and French rap as the night progresses. Oh, yes, those punch bowls … cups or jugs of the daily special are a gorgeously garnished bargain.

141

8 PANAME BREWING COMPANY

41 bis Quai de la Loire, 75019
01 40 36 43 55
www.panamebrewing
company.com
Open daily 11am–2am (lunch
12pm–3pm, dinner 6.30–11pm)
Metro Ourcq, Crimée
[MAP p. 186 C3]

'Paname' is pet slang for Paris,
but you might not exactly feel
like you're in Paris here (you'll
certainly be in no doubt you're
in a craft brewery, though).
A once rough and tumble
neighbourhood, servicing
the Bassin de la Villette, the
brewery's Quai de la Loire
home is now one of the city's
new fun zones and the Paname
pumps winter, summer and all
weathers inbetween. Massive
proportions and onsite brewing
lend it a utilitarian beauty and
steampunk vibe; five house
brews are fermented on site
in those big steel tanks. These
include an IPA (Barge du
Canal) and a formidable 6 per
cent dark and they also serve a
large number of fellow Parisian
craft brewers. The menu is
pub food, plain and simple:
pizzas, burgers, wings, falafel
and tacos. But you're here
for the beer, not to mention a
spot of people- and pleasure-
craft-watching on the massive,
floating terrace.

POCKET TIP

For dumplings in Belleville
try Guo Xin and Ravioli
Chinois Nord-Est or
head to Tunis-Tunis for
no-frill grills and Tunisian-
style couscous.

POCKET TIP

Rue de Bagnolet's Mama Shelter hotel put the 19th on everyone's radar; in summer their fun rooftop bar overlooks Paris' most scenic disused railway.

CHÂTEAU DE VERSAILLES

Louis XIV, known as Louis le Grand, or, most poetically, the Sun King, declared on his death bed, 'I depart, but the State shall always remain'. The French Revolution put an end to the absolute monarchs less than a hundred years later, but Louis' Château de Versailles, his gilded, glamourous renovation of a former hunting lodge, has indeed endured. If its symbolic expression of the divine right of Kings doesn't overwhelm, then its scale will, with 700 rooms to explore, 2000 windows to stare out of and 67 staircases to scamper up.

Versailles is the second most visited site in France, just after another of Louis XIV's pet projects, the Musée du Louvre (see p. 2). You'll never avoid the crowds but pre-purchase your ticket online to head straight to the security line; it's shortest before the tour buses descend around 10am and in the late afternoon. Visiting between October and May is quieter than in summer. Pre-booked guided tours also simplify entrance and give you access to the Mistresses Apartments. The château is open Tuesday to Sundays, the gardens are open every day and are free. All ticket price and seasonal opening hours information can be found online (www.en.chateauversailles.fr).

From stops across central Paris, it takes around 30 minutes on the RER C line to Versailles-Château Rive Gauche, from where it's a 10-minute walk to the Château itself. Staying in this ultra bourgeois and tourism-driven town can be an indulgence, given how easy it is to hop back on a Paris-bound train. But spreading your Versaille visit over two days can mean a more leisurely late afternoon experience at the Trianon, a dinner or evening performance and then fronting the château queues first thing the next morning.

CHÂTEAU DE VERSAILLES SIGHTS

If you only see one room, it must be the opulent **Galerie des Glaces** (Hall of Mirrors), a 75 metre-long ballroom lined with 17 enormous glittering mirrors on one side. The **Queen's Chamber**, refurbished by the ill-fated Marie Antoinette with fine Lyonnaise tapestries and a gilt balustrade is also a highlight, as is the chance to linger in the **L'Opera Royal** and the Gothic-style **Chapelle Royale** for an evening concert.

There's much to discover beyond the château. The **Domaine de Trianon** – the royal's home away from the château – offers a glimpse into their more personal tastes. Its **Grand Trianon** was where Louis XIV sought respite from court goings-on, while the **Petit Trianon**, built a century later, was where Louis XV entertained his mistress, the Comtesse Du Barry. The **Hameau de la Reine**, a mock-rustic village was built to indulge Marie Antoinette's fantasies of a simple life – it's where she infamously dressed as a milk maid.

Versaille's vast **gardens** are every bit as splendid as the château; Louis considered them as important and they were 40 years in the making. Their geometrical flower beds, paths, ponds, fountains, terraces and trees

POCKET TIP

Chapelle Royale and l'Opéra Royal are splendid, apt settings for the Baroque beauty of Handel, Bach or France's own Charpentier; evening performances happen year round.

from all over France, along with over 400 sculptures in bronze and marble, might be the pinnacle of formal French style, but they're relaxing to explore. To best admire the astonishing precision and grace of their design, known as the 'grand perspective', head to **water parterre** at the top of the **Latona Fountain** steps. In summer, fragrant Mediterranean citruses, palm and pomegranate trees, some more than 200 years old, are spread out across the **Orangerie**'s parterre. In winter, they're returned inside to shelter under 13-metre-high vaulted ceilings, protected from the cold by 4.5-metre walls. From April to October, the many fountains of the garden's exquisite groves and amphitheatres spurt and tinkle to an orchestral accompaniment.

Court life and costume drama takes a back seat to major works of contemporary art, specially commissioned each summer throughout the gardens and château. In the past, these have included a monumental waterfall tower by Olaf Eliasson and a series of large, provocative installations exploring Louis XIV's 'liberal' sexuality and absolute power by Anish Kapoor.

VERSAILLES EATING & DRINKING

The château gardens have a number of take-away places and small buvettes (outdoor bars), including a summertime sorbet stand. Superstar chef Alain Ducasse's **Ore** (Place D'Armes) is a new addition within the Pavillon Dufour, just inside the château's entrance. You'll enjoy stunning views from its floor-to-ceiling windows, with enough gilt accents among the pale grey and deep purple to help with post-palace bling-withdrawal. Breakfast or lunch can be scaled to fit any budget (or pre-book a set meal with château entrance included, to skip the ticket lines). There are also plenty of options a short walk into Versaille's centre. In town, lunch and dinner at the Michelin-starred **Le Table 11** (8 rue de la Chancellerie), is posh but far from stiff, in a pretty shopfront across from Cathédrale Saint-Louis de Versailles and is very reasonable if you opt for the daily set menu. For cool days and weary bones, bistrot à vins **Le Sept** (7 rue de Montreuil) serves simple hearty dishes like cassoulet or poulet roti, as well as a huge selection of organic wines. Collect supplies to take to dedicated picnic spots on the Saint Anthony Plain or by the Lake of the Swiss Guard, from the **Marché Notre-Dame** (Place du

Marché Notre-Dame) or lunch at one of the Marché Notre-Dame's small restaurants, like the **Cheese Club**. For a late afternoon pick-me-up wine, a plate of charcuterie and friendly, easy going staff, **No Water** (3 rue de Satory) is a local's favourite.

VERSAILLES SLEEPING

Hôtel Le Louis Versailles Château (2 bis avenue de Paris) is a glamourous, contemporary newcomer in a 19th-century building originally constructed for the War Ministry of Napoléon Bonaparte. Or live like a (soon to be guillotined) queen in old-fashioned luxury at **Trianon Palace Versailles** (1 boulevard de la Reine), fabulously positioned within the palace grounds. Prepare for frou-frou at **Hôtel de France** (5 rue Colbert) with matchy-matchy toile headboards and wallpaper, but you'll wake up but a few minutes' walk from the château. **Hôtel du Jeu de Paume** (5 bis rue de Fontenay), too is a short stroll away; rooms are simple and streamlined and there's a club-house style lounge to relax in.

POCKET TIP

Trianon Palace Versailles serves afternoon tea where you can sip Marie-Antoinette's favourite: a Ceylon blend scented with rose petals and apple from the château's kitchen garden.

LYON

This south-eastern city, a one time Gaulish 2nd-century AD powerhouse and 16th-century silk centre, is now considered France's gastronomic capital. Home of the bouchon – traditional restaurants that once catered to the city's silk workers – as well as the late, great Paul Bocuse, one of the country's greatest chefs, it's a place where deep culinary traditions are maintained while innovation and creativity also flourish. Despite being France's third-largest city, the pace is noticeably slower down here. Everyone has time for a long boozy lunch or an even longer degustation dinner (the Lyonnaise like to joke that there are three rivers in the city – the Rhône, the Saône and the Beaujolais wine). The nights too, stay balmy for longer. Its centre is compact: Roman ruins tumble down Fourvière Hill (*see* p. 152) and the UNESCO World Heritage listed Vieux Lyon is Europe's most extensive and pristine Renaissance neighbourhood. Beyond these thrillingly historic streets, the former docklands area of Confluence is where locals come to party and the city's future self evolves.

Lyon is ideal for an easy 24-hour getaway from Paris, but a daytrip lunch and wander is possible if you're short on time. There are almost hourly TGV trains from Paris Gare de Lyon to Lyon Part Dieu; it takes around two hours.

→ *Vieux Lyon's rooftops*

LYON SIGHTS

The funicular up Lyon's **Fourvière Hill** deposits you at the excellent Bernard Zehrfuss designed **Gallo-Roman Museum** (17 rue Cléberg) and the city's two incredibly well-preserved and still decorated **Roman theatres**, one dating back to 15 BCE. A short walk away is the 19th-century **Basilica of Notre-Dame de Fourvière** (8 Place de Fourvière), from where the views are stunning. There's Manets and Monets, Gauguins and Rodins, Picassos and Chagalls at the **Musée des Beaux-Arts** (20 Place des Terreaux) – an easy-going art viewing experience despite a collection that's second only to those in Paris. Confluence, a former docklands, is notable for its sustainable, sculptural architecture set in riverside parkland, and where you'll find good contemporary art galleries. At its **Musée des Confluences** (86 Quai Perrache), science-and anthropology-themed exhibitions are housed in a visually arresting building by Viennese postmodernists Coop Himmelb(l)au. Sights seen, leave time for simply taking in the atmosphere of the Renaissance alleys of **Vieux Lyon** and around hilltop silk-ateliers-cum-lofts, cool bars and cafes of **Croix-Rousse**.

LYON ∫HOPPING

Harking back to the city's silk days is the family-owned **L'Atelier de Soierie** (33 rue Romarin), which boasts France's last hand-silk-screening workshop and a range of scarves printed by the same team that turn out those for Hermès. But gourmet browsing is where Lyon really excels. **Les Halles de Lyon Paul Bocuse** (102 Cours Lafayette) has over 50 fresh produce or deli-like stalls over three floors, including **Charcuterie Sibilia**, famed throughout France for their pâtés en croute (pâté in pastry), terrines and andouillettes (coarse offal sausage), as well as more packable pastes and condiments. If you're peckish, and you will be, Les Halles de Lyon Paul Bocuse's also has sit-down concessions including **Chez Léon**, **Chez Les Gones** and **Le Fer à Cheval**. For a traditional outdoor produce market, **Le Marché de la Croix-Rousse** (boulevard de la Croix-Rousse), open Tuesday to Sunday, is the most delightful for a morning stroll and some saucisson (sausage) de Lyon or Saint Marcellin cheese. Fine textured and beautifully flavoured artisan chocolate can be found at **Bernachon** (42 Cours Franklin-Roosevelt), whose bonbons and bars are made with beans roasted right on the premises.

LYON EATING

Around 40 bouchons (traditional Lyonnais restaurants) have official accreditation: you'll see this displayed in their windows. Expect plenty of pork, including andouillettes and other offal sausages, along with quenelles (fish dumplings in shellfish sauce), cervelle de canut ('brains of the silk-weaver'; a herbed, garlicy cream cheese), hearty gratins and duck fat potatoes. **Daniel et Denise Saint Jean** (36 rue Tramassac), is pretty enough for a big night out, offers à la carte (many bouchons don't) and has staggeringly cheap wine by the carafe; while **Le Bouchon des Filles** (20 rue Sergent Blandan Ancienne Voie du Rhin) favours a lighter take on traditions. Michelin-stars also dot the city, with over 25 anointed restaurants, including the world's oldest three-star, Paul Bocuse's **L'Auberge du Pont** (40 rue de la Plage). Perpetually triple-starred since 1965, it's a fabulously over-the-top temple to the late, great chef and to his invention: nouvelle cuisine. Or discover some of the city's new generation chefs (known as the bande gourmandes) at **Les Apothicaires** (23 rue de Sèze), where a Bocuse and Noma trained pair mix global flavours and the region's magnificent produce.

LYON NIGHTLIFE & ꟻLEEPING

Lyon's electronic music scene is one of its lesser-known attractions. La Sucrière's rooftop **Le Sucre** (50 Quai Rambaud) is a lovely place for cocktail hour but also a great place to end your night with a late, late DJ set. **Sonic** (4 Quai des Étroits), a barge docked by the Quai des Étroits, hosts both experimental and rock acts.

The city also has some atmospheric places to stay across all budgets. For views to Mont Blanc, a pool and early 20th-century ocean liner look, **Villa Maïa** (8 rue Pierre Marion) is a luxurious aerie atop Fourvière Hill. The smart **OKKO Lafayette Lyon** (14 Bis Quai du General Sarrail) has a 24-hour club with complimentary snacks and apertifs, and its stylish Rhône-facing rooms all have bijou balconies. Across from Gare Saint-Paul station, the spartan chic rooms of the **Collège Hôtel** (5 Place Saint-Paul) come with vintage school desks and chairs, and 1930s' porthole windows that overlook the gorgeous Vieux Lyon rooftops. Super hostel **HO36** (36 rue Montesquieu) is in emerging riverside neighbourhood Guillotière; or the sprawling **Mob Hotel** (55 Quai Rambaud), with DJs and an organic restaurant, is in the middle of the Confluence action.

POCKET TIP

La Sucrière's rooftop Le Sucre (50 Quai Rambaud) is home to the annual Nuits Sonores electronic music festival in late May.

155

CHAMPAGNE

East of Paris is the region famed for its namesake: Champagne. So rich is the region's wine culture that its key vineyards and cellars were granted a UNESCO world heritage listing in 2015. There are more than one hundred Champagne maisons (houses), along with cooperatives and vignerons (artisan producer/growers), spread across five sub-regions. These range from the famous multinational-owned brands who buy-in their grapes, to family run concerns on tiny parcels of land. All adhere to strict standards of production to call their product Champagne. Tastings and tours are held by the grand houses that dot the city of Reims. Champagne's unofficial capital, Épernay, is also packed with both big name houses and small wine bars, especially along avenue de Champagne. Vineyard wandering and getting to know the smaller growers can take a little more organisation but can make for a wonderful couple of days' driving. For daytrippers wanting a break from the bubbles, head to Reims (see p. 159), a fascinating, richly historical city, with some nice non-liquid diversions.

Reims is only 45 minutes from Paris' Gare de l'Est on the TGV train, and there are direct 30-minute connections to and from Charles De Gaulle Airport to Gare Champagne-Ardenne. Far smaller, Épernay is around a 15-minute train ride on from Reims.

→ Champagne village and vines

POCKET TIP

Roman lime mining and a medieval chalk boom gave Reims a network of subterranean chambers called crayères (cellars). Canny Madame Clicquot discovered these are perfect for gently aging Champagne.

CHAMPAGNE TASTE

Almost none of the houses accept walk-ins, so plan your visit ahead of time and book online. In Reims, veritable **Ruinart** (www.ruinart.com), dating back to 1768, has the deepest and most atmospheric of crayères (cellars), so ancient as to be classified as a national monument. **Veuve Clicquot** (www.veuveclicquot.com), the second-largest house in the region, and known for their Pinot Noir-focussed blends, is also a historical treat – opt for the 'In the footsteps of Madame Clicquot' tour. **Taittinger** (www.taittinger.com) has 4-kilometres (2.4 miles) of crayères that are open to tour, along with custom-designed tastings. Thirty small-grower Champagnes are represented at wine shop and tasting room, **Trésors de Champagne** (www.boutique-tresors-champagne.com).

Épernay's grand houses all line up along its beautiful avenue de Champagne. **Moët & Chandon** (www.moet.com) offer a number of tours in their particularly spooky 27 kilometres (16 miles) of tunnels, each focussing on a different Champagne style. **Mercier** (www.champagnemercier.com), a Champagne well known and loved in France, also has an extensive underground network of cellars; it's so sprawling that there's a small train to help you get around.

POCKET TIP

If you'd prefer to maximise tasting time, or you haven't booked a tour, Michel Gonet (www.gonet.fr), with a fairytale villa and garden on Épernay's avenue de Champagne, allows you to do just that.

CHAMPAGNE SIGHTS

Reims is a richly historical city that can provide an afternoon diversion from the real reason you're in the region. The **Musée de la Reddition** (12 rue du Roosevelt), the site of Germany's World War II surrender, is small, but its 'war room' – 1940s' maps and all – is wholly preserved in its original state. All French coronations were held at the **Notre-Dame de Reims** (Place du Luçon) for a thousand years, its Gothic splendour the backdrop when Jeanne d'Arc headed up the procession for Charles VII. Despite the fact Chagall's stained-glass windows only date back to last century – they replaced the originals destroyed after shells rained down upon the town in 1914 – the artist's luminescent blues are as sublime and other-worldly as the surrounding architecture.

With a few days to explore, head down the Côte des Blancs, 100 kilometres (62 miles) from Épernay, to medieval **Sézanne**, its rolling hills planted with Chardonnay grapes. 'This little city of character' has a lovely medieval heart and 410 linden trees. While there, you may as well try the Chardonnay-based Champagnes from the surrounding, relatively new **Cotes de Sézanne**. Then head further to **Troyes**, for its streets of higgledy-piggledy

half-timbered houses dating to the 14th century. In between, wander the glorious open gardens of **Baconnes**, an historic village-fleuri (flower village).

CHAMPAGNE EATING

Don't come to Champagne for neo-bistro smarts or cheap eats: when drinking the world's most highly finessed sparklings, most will want to pair that with Michelin-level dining. Still, if you just fancy a quick plate of oysters and, well, Champagne, head to **Le Bocal** at Reim's fish market, with a short menu of coquillages, crustacés and smoked fish. For unpretentious French provincial dishes and a great value 'market' menu, try **Brasserie du Boulingrin** (31 rue de Mars, Reims). Reims is also known for its blushing sweet, crisp biscuit roses de Reims, which you can pick up at **Maison Fossier** (2 rue Maurice Prévoteau, Reims). If you are on a dedicated gourmet pilgrimage, Reims' most in-demand tables are at the elegant **L'Assiette Champenoise** (40 avenue Paul Vaillant-Couturier, Tinqueux), with three Michelin stars and boasting one of France's best young chefs, while the Domaine Les Crayères' opulent **Le Parc** (64 boulevard Henry Vasnier, Reims) has two stars. Both do fine dining's signature

deconstructed plates, though both honour local, seasonal ingredients and traditional French technique too. In Épernay, you can order groaning charcuterie and cheese platters to accompany excellent small-grower Champagnes at simple and central **C-Comme**.

CHAMPAGNE SLEEPING

Basic B&Bs dot the region, but if you're here to sleep in style, there are some magnificent options. Overlooking Reims, the fetching, fairytale-like **Château de Sacy** (rue des Croisettes, Sacy) sits among vineyards and has a handful of pretty but nicely pared-back, individually decorated rooms, some with circular baths and all with picturesque views. Its restaurant **Le Vigny** is also well regarded. Ten minutes north of Épernay, the **Royal Champagne** (9 rue de la République–Hameau de Bellevue, Champillon), has luxurious, contemporary rooms and a hugely glamourous fine dining restaurant. The intimate, smart **Hôtel Restaurant les Avisés**, part of **Domaine Jacques Selosse** (59 rue de Cramant, Avize), is around 15-minutes drive from the centre of Épernay, offering tastings of Champagne so sought after that bottles are indented from year to year.

GETTING TO PARIƧ

ARRIVING BY AIR

Charles De Gaulle (CDG)

Paris' major international airport – often referred to by locals as Roissy – is around 30 kilometres (18.6 miles) north-east of the city centre. There are three terminals: 1, 2 & 3. A free light rail, **CDGVAL**, connects all three terminals. Terminal 2 has several sub-terminals: A to G, which are all connected internally, apart from (very) remote 2G. A free shuttle runs to 2G runs from 2F.

RER trains run to Gare du Nord and Châtelet les Halles (from where you can connect to the Metro) between 5am and midnight and cost €10.30. The RER B station is located between terminals 2C/2D and 2F/2E or for Terminal 1, Roissypole. These are regular commuter routes, and it's wise to be on guard against thieves, especially in peak hour.

RoissyBus costs €12 and runs from all terminals at CDG to Paris (Opéra); **Le Bus Direct** (www.lebusdirect.com) replaces the old Air France airport service, with half-hourly coaches leaving to Étoile and Port Maillot metro stops (€18) and Gare Montparnasse and Gare du Lyon stations (€18), both take between one and one and a half hours.

Orly

Paris' second airport is 18 kilometres (11 miles) south of Paris. Flights to and from here are mostly domestic, intra-European or to North Africa. There are two terminals: Sud (south) and Ouest (west). It's closer in than CDG but is frankly a pain to get to by public transport.

RER B and RER C trains connect to Orly via a shuttle train, Orlyval, and a bus service respectively; transfer onto the Orlyval at Antony station. RER B/Orlyval costs €12.50, and RER C/bus costs €6.80.

OrlyBus (€8.70) leave every 8–15 minutes to Denfert-Rochereau, or to Eiffel Tower and Montparnasse (€12); there is also a shuttle between CDG and Orly (€22).
Le Bus Direct runs to Étoile and Champs-Élyseées (€12)

Information on driving routes, terminals and airlines can be found at www.aeroportsdeparis.fr

Airport Taxis

Taxis to and from CDG take around 30–60 minutes, depending on the time of day and cost a flat fee of €50/€55 (Left Bank/Right Bank), while those to Orly take 20–40 minutes and cost €30/€35 (Right Bank/Left Bank). Luggage attracts a €1 surcharge per piece. At the airport, do not accept lifts from drivers who approach you – registered taxi drivers will never do this.

Uber can be booked either way (around €45 to or from CDG or Orly), though pick-ups are not as seamless as for a normal taxi.
G7 taxis (www.g7.fr) can be booked online in English, or if you call there are English speaking operators.

ARRIVING BY TRAIN

Eurostar (www.eurostar.com) services from London and **Thalys** (www.thalys.com) services from Brussels, Antwerp, Amsterdam and Cologne arrive and depart from Gare du Nord. France's national train service **SNCF** (www.sncf.com), which has both domestic and international routes and includes the fast TGV network, arrives into various stations: Gare du Nord, Gare du Montparnasse, Gare de l'Est, Gare du Lyon, Bercy, Austerlitz and Gare Saint-Lazare.

GETTING AROUND PARIƧ

Walking

Distances in Paris are often far smaller than they may appear on maps and as Paris' traffic snarls are often so bad, it can be quicker, and far less stressful, to walk than take a taxi.

Public Transport

Public transport – Metro, buses, the RER, trams and the Montmartre funicular – in

Paris and its suburbs is run by government company **RATP** (www.ratp.fr). The website has dedicated information for tourists in several languages and links to download their itinerary app: Next Stop Paris.

Ticketing

All of the below can be bought at ticket windows and machines at metro and RER stations.

RATP's Paris Visite travel card is valid for 1, 2, 3 or 5 consecutive days in zones 1–3 (€12/€19.50/€26.65/€38.35) or 1–5 (includes CDG or Orly and Disneyland Paris and Château de Versailles, €25.25/€38.35/€53.75/€65.80). Depending on which zones you choose, it covers all metro travel, RER lines, Transilien SNCF buses, RATP and Optile buses throughout the Ile-de-France, Orlyval and the Montmartre funicular.

If you're planning a day of sightseeing in Paris itself, **Mobilis** card is a better deal at €7.50 per day, and if you're here for a few weeks, or plan to return to Paris often (it happens!), a **Navigo** card (€22.80/€75.20 weekly/monthly) will save you money and is relatively straightforward to buy; you'll just need a passport-sized photo.

Single trip T+ tickets (€1.90) can also be used across the system and can be purchased singly or in packs of ten (adult/concession €14.90/€7.45) from metro stations or directly from drivers on buses.

Metro

Metro trains run frequently between 5.30am and 1am, or to 2am on Friday and Saturdays. Intersecting lines are colour coded and numbered – there are 14 in total. It's a good idea to remember the name of the last station in the direction you are going, as this is sometimes the only signage displayed in metro station corridors. RATP's Visiting Paris by Metro app is available for free from the website and most hotels and department stores have free official metro maps.

Bus

Paris Transilien bus network can be daunting but provides handy shortcuts across the city (plus you get to see the sights, unlike on the metro). Route stops are marked at each bus stop and on buses. At night, when the metro is closed, the **Noctilien** service takes over. Night buses run every 10–30 minutes and fan out from Châtelet, Montparnasse, Gare de l'Est, Gare Saint-Lazare, and Gare de Lyon. See: www.rapt.fr for specific routes and timetables.

RER

Five express train lines connect the city centre to surrounding suburbs, and within Paris they function as an express option.

Vélib (bike share)

The city's popular bike share system is one of the world's most extensive. The chunky grey bikes, over 14,500 of them, along with new electric models, can be collected and returned to any of the 1000+ docking stations. One day/one week passes cost €5/€15, and the first 30 minutes are free. Subscribe online in advance (www.velibmetropole.fr) or at machines at any docking station. Note, the system has been glitchy of late, with bike-less racks not uncommon, so have a back-up plan.

Batobus

Batobus (www.batobus.com.) tourist boat along the Seine has stops close to many of Paris' major attractions. It's a hop-on-hop-off service: one-/two-day passes cost €17/€19.

Taxi & Ridesharing

Paris' taxis are cheap by European standards but can be hard to find especially at peak hour or on weekend evenings. Rooftop lights are green when a taxi is free, red when it's taken, although they won't stop if you are within 50 metres of a taxi stand. There is a minimum charge of €7 – it's not unusual to pay little more than that. **G7** (www.g7.fr) is the largest company and has a dedicated English line if you want to book. Bonus: they also have in-taxi wi-fi and magazines. **Uber** is popular, if occasionally unreliable, in Paris. There is a similar local service called **Le Cab** (www.lecab.fr); unlike taxis they don't have a minimum spend so are good for super short hops.

Private Drivers

There are plenty of private car services in Paris, but for added charm and a personal guide, try **Cedric's Paris** (www.cedricsparis.com), where you'll be whisked around the city in a vintage Citroën 2CV, or for groups, a VW Combi.

EATING OUT

France has set meal times that are followed by restaurants, although this has begun to change in Paris with a number of service continu – places that either serve full meals all day or at least a menu of sizeable snacks between lunch and dinner services. Otherwise, dinner will rarely be available before 7pm, and most Parisians don't dine before 8pm, often much later. Don't hesitate to eat earlier – it's when you can nab a table at an otherwise hard-to-book place – or follow the local custom of taking an apéro before dinner.

Many restaurants offer cheaper fixed price lunches and dinners, either a two or three (or more) course 'menu' or 'une formule' (a menu with no choice of courses). These give you either no or limited choice per course but are usually great value. Note that some dishes, usually because of a particular ingredient, will incur an additional charge or supplement, marked with a +. While the French can be rigid about adhering to the traditional three-course meal structure, a more casual small plate dining experience has become hugely popular in Paris of late.

It's considered bad form to request changes to dishes based on likes and dislikes. You are there to eat what the chef – a highly regarded professional – has prepared. That said, restaurant staff are increasingly aware of food intolerances and will often be able to suggest a dish that is suitable or perhaps make minor modifications.

Paris' waiters have been long known for their surliness but there's a new breed of staff that are unfailingly charming and helpful. Be respectful and polite whatever the case. You'll also notice Parisians rarely get rowdy at restaurants, and loud conversation or raucous laughter may attract disapproving stares.

Restaurants sometimes offer an excellent childrens' menu for €10–15, with a choice of either meat, say a minute steak, or simple grilled fish served with vegetables or fries, a small dessert and mineral water with mint or raspberry syrup. If not, it's fine to ask if child-size portions are available.

You'll usually need to ask for the bill (l'addition, s'il vous plaît) when you are finished. Service charges are included, so tipping is not obligatory. But a tip of anything from 5–10%, or rounding up in more casual places, will be appreciated (and can be wise if you intend to return).

USEFUL EATING & DRINKING TERMS

à point/saignant: medium rare/rare, for steak.

apéro: both noun and verb in English, taking a pre-dinner drink or aperitif.

biologique or bio: organic.

bistro, bistrot: a small restaurant, though also refers to the traditional style of cuisine served.

cave à vin/caves à manger/bistrot a vin: wine shop/wine shop and bar with casual food/wine bar with a full menu.

neo-bistrot/bistronomic: contemporary, informal restaurants, usually offering innovative reworkings of traditional dishes.

pichet: carafe; a quart (250ml) or demi (500ml).

pression: draft beer on tap.

terrace: footpath or courtyard tables.

zinc bar: 'le zinc' – steel topped counter in a bar and the bar itself; a friendly local, similar to 'pub' in English.

COFFEE

Paris' many 'third-wave' or Anglo-style cafes usually serve coffee with a similar nomenclature to their counterparts in the US, Australia and the UK.

Traditional French coffee terminology still holds sway in neighbourhood bars and more traditional cafes and includes:

le café au lait: coffee with milk.

un café crème, un crème: espresso with hot milk; like a cafe latte, but usually weaker.

un café noisette, une noisette: espresso with a dash of milk or a spoonful of foam, similar to a macchiato.

un café américain, café noir, café allongé: long black, weak black coffee.

déca, Hag: the suffix for decaf coffee (Hag is a brand).

café Cognac: booze-laden short black.

ETIQUETTE

Parisians have a reputation for reserve and old fashion civilities are still the norm: politeness can really work in your favour. Always extend a 'bonjour madame/monsieur (hello)' and 'au revoir (goodbye)' or 'merci (thank you)' to everyone from shop assistants to taxi drivers to someone you ask for directions. Do try and use whatever French you have, even if it is just a few words, though also expect, unless you are truly fluent, for a large percentage of Parisians to quickly switch the conversation back to English.

POST

We've all been there: a quick spot of shopping and suddenly you've got a suitcase that's bursting its zips or, worse, baggage allowance blues at the airport. **La Poste** – the national post office, and easy to find across Paris – sells reasonably priced prepaid international Colissimo boxes (www.colissimo.fr) for 5kg or 7kg, they're trackable and can be insured.

SHOPPING

Until recently shops in Paris followed strict opening hours with everything closed on Sundays. This still holds sway but shopping zones like those in the Marais, Le Halle, boulevard Haussmann and avenue Montaigne are now exempt, and open on Sunday afternoons. Supermarket hours vary, but smaller branches often remain open on Sundays too.

Parisians are still devoted to their local produce markets, where stalls sell fresh produce, cheese, meat and flowers. Most are open one or two mornings each week, though some open daily.

There are two country-wide national sales periods of six weeks each, the 'soldes d'hiver' in January/February and the 'soldes d'été' in June/July. The official dates can change year to year and can be found online. Sale discounts usually begin at 30–50%, but can hit 70% during the last weeks.

PUBLIC HOLIDAYS

There are 11 public holidays throughout the year in France. Most museums will be closed on New Year's Day, Christmas day, Labour Day on May 1 and Assumption Day on August 15. The French like to 'fare le pont', literally 'to do or make a bridge', taking the days off in between public holidays to make extra long weekends. There are four public holidays in May – these are sometimes strung together to make longer holidays, called the 'les ponts de mai' (and why May weekends in Paris can feel quieter than usual and transport out of the city is heavily booked).

WHAT TO WEAR

One constant in Paris is the idea of looking effortless. This does not for a second mean *not* making an effort, rather it means seeming (the key word) like you are not trying too hard. Sports clothes, flip-flops or jogging shoes will of course mark you out immediately as a tourist, but so will the opposite, i.e. over the top head-to-toe label displays and overtly sexy style. Does it matter? Looking vaguely the part really does go down well and know that many a fashionable Parisian mixes good-quality basics, say a trench or blazer, with jeans and pieces from local mid-price labels, vintage shops and even supermarket chain Monoprix. They also see little problem wearing essentially the same outfit every day, everywhere.

PHARMACIES

French pharmacies – always marked with a green cross – can often offer advice and have a far larger range of over-the-counter medicines for minor health problems than those in Anglophone countries; if your closest pharmacy is closed, there will be a list on the door of those nearby that are open on weekends and late at night. A reliable, central 24-hour option is Pharmacie de la Place de la République (5 Place de la Republique, 3e), who also stock skincare lines La Roche-Posay, Nuxe, Avène, Darphin and Bioderma.

EMERGENCIES

The phone number for police, ambulance and fire is 112.

TOILETS

Paris has over 400 self-cleaning public toilets, which are free and wheelchair accessible. These can be found near most major tourist attractions and there is an up-to-date list on the **City of Paris** website (www.paris.fr). Department stores, major hotels and fast food chains are other good options. If you are busting to go and can't find a public facility, don't chance using those in a bar without first buying a Perrier or espresso.

TOURIST INFORMATION

The City of Paris' tourist information centre is **Paris Rendevous** (www.boutique. paris.fr; 29 rue de Rivoli, 4th, Mon–Sat 10am–7pm, Métro Hôtel de Ville, Châtelet). It has a large range of maps and guides, a shop of French-made gifts and wi-fi. The **Paris Convention and Visitors Bureau** (www.en.parisinfo.com) has information, including concert and events and a booking service.

WI-FI

Cafes and bars often offer free, passworded wi-fi (pronounced 'whi-fee') and the free **Paris Wi-fi** service is available in around 300 public places, including parks, major squares and libraries. There's a map and list at the **City of Paris** website (www.paris.fr).

PARIS

17ᴱ

GRANDES
CARRIÈRES

172-3 ────

PARC
MONCEAU ⊕

FONDATION ⊕
LOUIS VUITTON

174-5

8ᴱ

PORTE-
DAUPHINE

CHAMPS-
ELYSÉES

RÉCIPROQUE
⊕

16ᴱ

7ᴱ

INVALIDE

AUTEUIL

CRAVAN
○

MARCHÉ
SAXE- ⊕
BRETEUIL

182

NOTRE-DAME
DES-CHAMPS

15ᴱ

193

14ᴱ

192

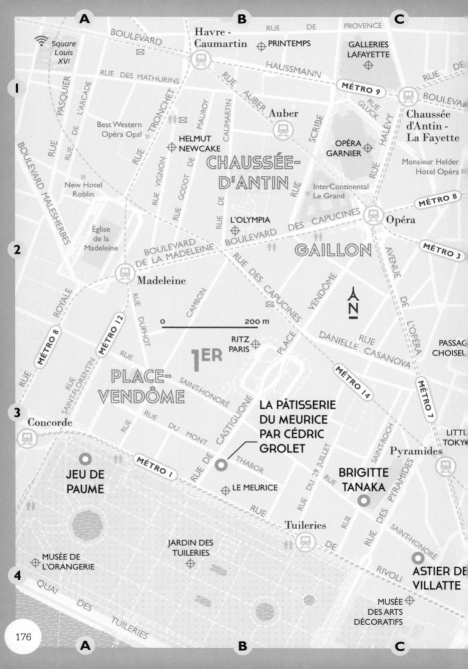

D

E

F

Colonel
Fabien

PAVILLON
PUEBLA

I

AVENUE

SIMÓN   BOLÍVAR

AUX BELLES

VELLEFAUX

BOULEVARD

LE FONTAINE
DE BELLEVILLE

0   200 m

RÉBEVAL

DE LA GRANGE

CLAUDE

MÉTRO 2

Square
Rébeval

RUE

HÔPITAL-
SAINT-LOUIS

DE

GUO
XIN

Jardin
de l'Hôpital
Saint-Louis

AVENUE

RUE SAINT-MAUR

LA

VILLETTE

BELLEVILLE

RAVIOLI
CHINOIS
NORD-EST

RUE   DE

LE COMPTOIR
GÉNÉRAL

Belleville

LE GRAND
BAIN

LE PETIT
GRAIN

2

RAMPONEAU

N

RUE

BICHAT

LA JAVA

DU   TEMPLE

BOULEVARD

TUNIS-
TUNIS

RUE

GALERIE
SULTANA

FAUBOURG

Square
Jules Verne

DE

L'ORILLON

DE

RUE DU

Goncourt

MIZNON

AVENUE

Église
Saint-Joseph
des Nations

RUE

AU

ROI

LE COMMUNE
PUNCH CLUB

Couronnes

Square du
Nouveau
Belleville

MÉTRO 11

RUE

DE

LA

FONTAINE

RUE DES TROIS

COURONNES

3

BELLEVILLE

BOULEVARD JULES FERRY

FOLIE-
MÉRICOURT

RUE   DES   TROIS

BORNES

PARMENTIER

SAINTMAUR

RUE

MORET

L'INTERNATIONAL

OBERKAMPF

AVENUE

RUE   DES   TROIS

MÉTRO 3

DE

BOULEVARD RICHARD LENOIR

Parmentier

LA

RUE

Hôtel
Verlain

Rue
Saint-Maur

BOULEVARD

VOLTAIRE

LE VERRE VOLÉ
CAVE À VINS

CHAMBELLAND

RÉPUBLIQUE

4

Filles du
Calvaire

Oberkampf

CLOWN
BAR

LE VERRE VOLÉ
ÉPICERIE ET
SANDWICHERIE

AVENUE PARMENTIER

SAINT-
AMBROISE

LIBRARIE
YVON LAMBERT

CAFÉ
MÉRICOURT

179

D

E

F

Square du Temple-Elie Wiesel

Hôtel Picard

GRAND CAFÉ TORTONI

MARCHE DES ENFANTS ROUGES

FABIEN BREUVART PHOTOGRAPHY

Filles du Calvaire

CLOWN BAR

Oberkampf

LE VERRE VOLÉ CAVE À VINS

LE VERRE VOLÉ ÉPICERIE ET SANDWICHERIE

LIBRAIRIE YVON LAMBERT

PASSAGE SAINT-PIERRE AMELOT

PASSAGE SAINT-SÉBASTIEN

AU PASSAGE

CARBÓN PARIS

BOOT

St-Sébastien - Froissart

Saint Sébastien (hotel)

GALERIE PERROTIN

MERCI

RUE AMELOT

Richard Lenoir

2

sée Archives ionales

BREIZH CAFÉ ODEON

CAFÉ LA PERLE

Centre Culturel Suisse

MAISON PLISSON

ARCHIVES

OLIVIA CLERGUE

Square Léopold Achille

Jardin s Rosiers – oh-Migneret

FRAGMENTS

SAINT-GILLES

Chemin Vert

BENSIMON HOME AUTOUR DU MONDE

Bréguet-Sabin

3

int-Paul

Hôtel Emile

Église Saint-Paul-Saint-Louis

0   200 m

VIN DES PYRÉNÉES & LE 1905

MÉTRO 5

MÉTRO 8

MÉTRO 1

Bastille

4

181

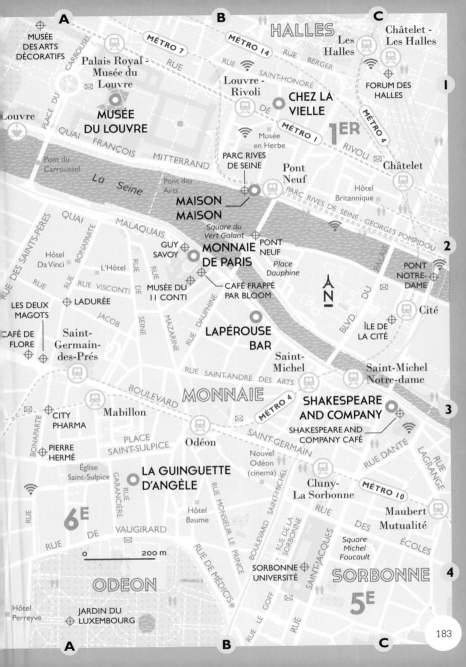

MUSÉE
DES ARTS
DÉCORATIFS

Palais Royal -
Musée du
Louvre

MÉTRO 7

MÉTRO 14

RUE

HALLES

Les
Halles

Châtelet -
Les Halles

RUE   BERGER

RUE   SAINT-HONORÉ

Louvre -
Rivoli

**CHEZ LA
VIELLE**

FORUM DES
HALLES

1ER

I

Louvre

MÉTRO 4

CARROUSEL

PLACE DU

**MUSÉE
DU LOUVRE**

QUAI   FRANÇOIS   MITTERRAND

Musée en Herbe

MÉTRO 1

RIVOLI

Châtelet

**PARC RIVES
DE SEINE**

Pont du
Carrousel

Pont des
Arts

La Seine

Pont
Neuf

Hôtel
Britannique

PARC RIVES DE SEINE - GEORGES POMPIDOU

**MAISON
MAISON**

Square du
Vert Galant

GUY
SAVOY

**MONNAIE
DE PARIS**

**PONT
NEUF**

Place
Dauphine

**PONT
NOTRE-
DAME**

2

QUAI DES SAINTS-PÈRES

QUAI   MALAQUAIS

BONAPARTE

Hôtel
Da Vinci

L'Hôtel

RUE

RUE

RUE VISCONTI

RUE DE

**CAFÉ FRAPPÉ
PAR BLOOM**

N

DU   PALAIS

BLVD

Cité

**MUSÉE DU
11 CONTI**

ÎLE
DE
LA CITÉ

LADURÉE

JACOB

SEINE

MAZARINE

RUE DAUPHINE

**LAPÉROUSE
BAR**

Saint-
Michel

Saint-Michel
Notre-dame

**LES DEUX
MAGOTS**

CAFÉ DE
FLORE

Saint-
Germain-
des-Prés

RUE   SAINT-ANDRÉ   DES   ARTS

MONNAIE

MÉTRO 4

**SHAKESPEARE
AND COMPANY**

3

CITY
PHARMA

BOULEVARD

Mabillon

SAINT-GERMAIN

SHAKESPEARE AND
COMPANY CAFÉ

RUE DANTE

RUE
LAGRANGE

BONAPARTE

PIERRE
HERMÉ

PLACE
SAINT-SULPICE

Odéon

Nouvel
Odéon
(cinema)

MÉTRO 10

Cluny-
La Sorbonne

**Maubert
Mutualité**

Église
Saint-Sulpice

**LA GUINGUETTE
D'ANGÈLE**

RUE GARANCIÈRE

Hôtel
Baume

RUE MONSIEUR LE PRINCE

BOULEVARD SAINT-MICHEL

RUE DE LA
SORBONNE

RUE

DES

ÉCOLES

Square
Michel Foucault

RUE

6E

DE

VAUGIRARD

RUE

RUE DE MÉDICIS

0   200 m

ODÉON

SORBONNE
UNIVERSITÉ

RUE   LE   GOFF

RUE SAINT-JACQUES

SORBONNE

5E

4

Hôtel
Perreyve

JARDIN DU
LUXEMBOURG

183

A   B   C

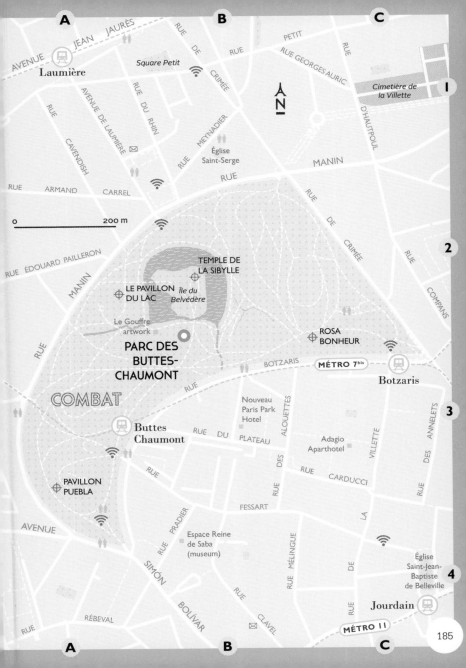

18E

Rosa Parks 🚇

Square Curial

N

RUE DE L'ÉVANGILE

RUE

RUE CURIAL

PASSAGE WATTIEAUX

RUE

GASTON

TESSIER

CAMBRAI

DE FLANDRE

RUE LABOIS-ROUILLON

RUE RAYMOND RADIGUET

Hôtel Paris Villette ✉

RUE DE CRIMÉE

L'OURC

VILLETTE

Hôtel Crimée

AVENUE

✉ 📶

RUE CURIAL

MATHIS

Crimée 🚇

RUE DE JOINVILLE

CAFÉ-CACHÉ ⊕ **LE 104** ◉

MAISON DES PETITS ⊕ ⊕

RUE D'AUBERVILLIERS

RUE ARCHEREAU

RUE

Jardin de l'îlot Riquet

RUE DE CRIMÉE

Gresset (hotel)

Église Saint-Jacques Saint-Christop

GRAND CENTRAL

RUE

RIQUET

FLANDRE

RUE DUVERGIER

Les Jardins d'Éole

RUE D'AUBERVILLIERS

RUE TANGER

RUE SUZANNE MASSON

Riquet ✉ 🚇

RUE

RIQUET

SEINE

RUE DE ROUEN

LA

PANAME BREWING COMPAN

📶

Jardin Luc-Hoffmann

RUE DE

MÉTRO 1

PASSAGE DE FLANDRE

DE

QUAI

LA LOIRE

Bassin de la Villette

◉

📶 PARIS PLAGE

RUE

MAROC

📶

Horizons Suspendus sculpture

⊕

Square du quai de la Loire

Square Marcel Mouloudji

📶

Laumière 🚇

AVENUE

BASSIN DE LA VILLETTE

QUAI

DE

Hôtel Ibis Budget

JAURÈS

MEAUX

RUE CAVENDISH

LAUR

Stalingrad 🚇

JEAN

AVENUE

✉

RUE

DE

186

A   B   C

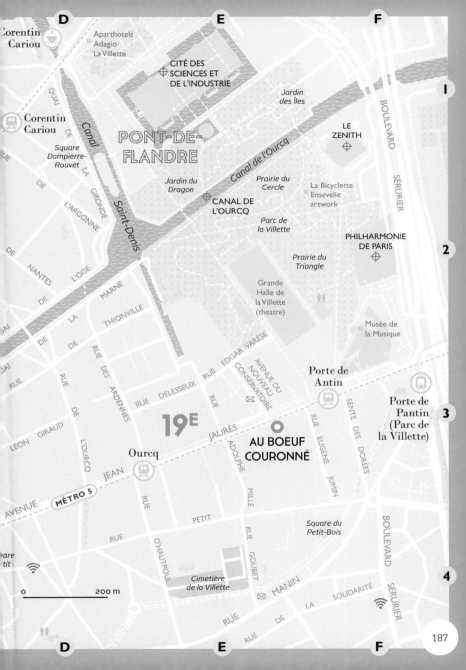

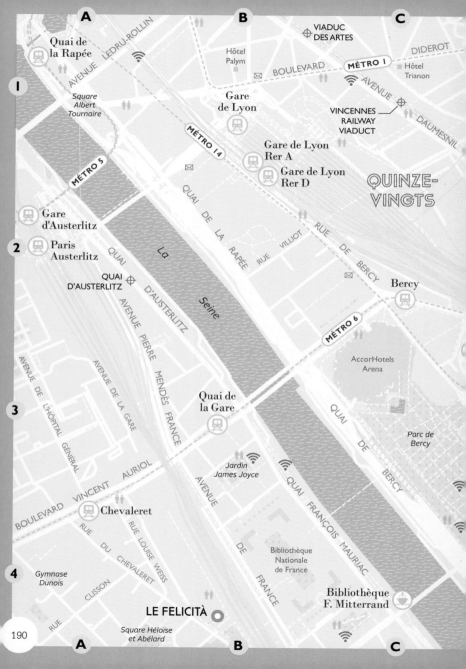

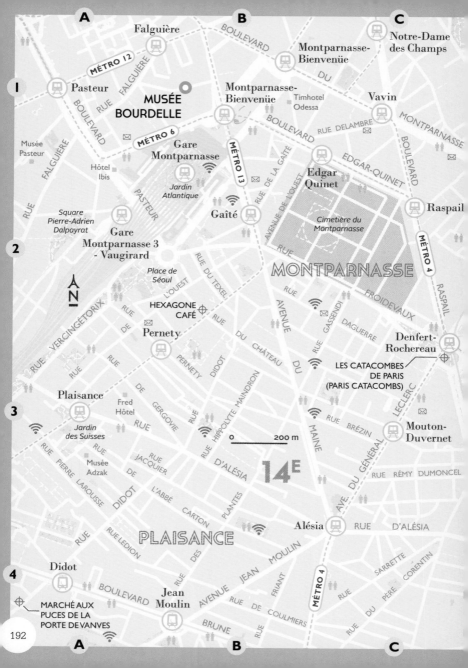

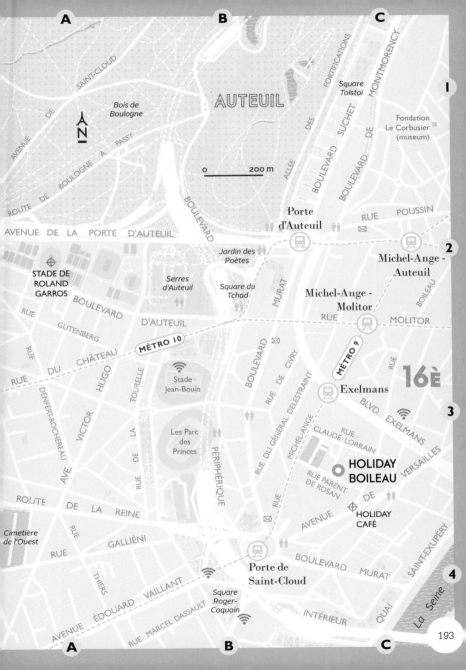

INDEX

ABOUT THE AUTHOR

Paris was the first place I visited beyond my native Australia. Not long out of art school, it was a life-changing trip: full of swoons, both literal and figurative, where I drank in the Delacroixs, not to mention the clafouti and couscous and Chablis, pawed Clergerie shoes I couldn't afford, danced to MC Solaar in the 11th, went to Algerian raï concerts, and spent endless hours name checking everything I'd ever read in Zola and Camus, Duras, Beckett and Benjamin, everything I'd ever seen in Truffault, Godard, Rohmer and Marker films. It's also, poignantly, the only city where I've nursed a broken heart.

After a long absence, I returned in 2006 and have since been both visitor and resident. Paris has also been a base while working on guidebooks and other travel and culture assignments in France, North Africa, Italy, Portugal, Belgium, Austria and Norway, and a welcome second home when living across the border in Turin. I've never lost the giddy sense of delight that marked my first stay, but breathless fascination has grown into enduring love, as I've come to know the city in its many moods, to understand its nuances and complexities.

ACKNOWLEDGEMENTS

For thirty years, I've found Parisians warm, unfailingly kind and gracious in sharing their city and lives. Big smoochy bises to the le Baron Rouge crew (everyday is a Muscadet!); Laura Lot for the company, care and comps; Caryl Phillips and Glyn Maxwell for indulging me that terrible St-Germain bar; Luke Davies for the boudin noir and Jacque Réda; Gabrielle Lubtchansky for great local tips; Cenk Boduroglu for 19th drinks; Karl Geary for breaking your writerly solitude; July Bigot for a wonderful list and invites; Fabrice Delaneau for convivial company and Marais insight; Kylie Ruszczynski for respite and conversation; Andreas Carerre for the Licher and late night tunes; Olivier-Paul Nirlo for that epic ride up the Butte and dance floor debauch; Justin Westover, for always knowing the words and 11th-hour succour. In Melbourne, to Alice Barker for astute and sensitive editing, suggestions and contributions, publisher Melissa Kayser, designer Michelle Mackintosh and Megan Ellis for fabulous series vision, and, finally, to Joe, Rumer and Biba Guario, for allowing me a life I never imagined possible.

PHOTO CREDITS

Some of the material in this book originally appeared in Paris Precincts, published by Explore Australia Publishing Pty Ltd, 2016, where full acknowledgements for individual contributions appear.

Published in 2019 by Hardie Grant Travel, a division of Hardie Grant Publishing

Hardie Grant Travel (Melbourne)
Building 1, 658 Church Street
Richmond, Victoria 3121

Hardie Grant Travel (Sydney)
Level 7, 45 Jones Street
Ultimo, NSW 2007

www.hardiegrant.com/au/travel

The maps in this publication incorporate data from © OpenStreetMap contributors.

OpenStreetMap is made available under the Open Database Licence: http://opendatacommons.org/licences/odbl/1.0/. Any rights in individual contents of the database are licensed under the Database Contents Licence: http://opendatacommons.org/licenses/dcbl/1.0/

A catalogue record for this book is available from the National Library of Australia

Paris Pocket Precincts
ISBN 9781741176308

10 9 8 7 6 5 4 3 2 1

Publisher
Melissa Kayser

Senior editor
Megan Cuthbert

Project editor
Alice Barker

Editorial assistance
Rosanna Dutson

Proofreader
Helena Holmgren

Cartography
Jason Sankovic, Emily Maffei

Cartographic research
Claire Johnston

Design
Michelle Mackintosh

Typesetting
Megan Ellis

Index
Max McMaster

Prepress
Megan Ellis and Splitting Image Colour Studio

Printed and bound in China by LEO Paper Group

Disclaimer: While every care is taken to ensure the accuracy of the data within this product, the owners of the data (including the state, territory and Commonwealth governments of Australia) do not make any representations or warranties about its accuracy, reliability, completeness or suitability for any particular purpose and, to the extent permitted by law, the owners of the data disclaim all responsibility and all liability (including without limitation, liability in negligence) for all expenses, losses, damages (including indirect or consequential damages) and costs which might be incurred as a result of the data being inaccurate or incomplete in any way and for any reason.

Publisher's Disclaimers: The publisher cannot accept responsibility for any errors or omissions. The representation on the maps of any road or track is not necessarily evidence of public right of way. The publisher cannot be held responsible for any injury, loss or damage incurred during travel. It is vital to research any proposed trip thoroughly and seek the advice of relevant government and travel bodies before you leave.

Publisher's Note: Every effort has been made to ensure that the information in this book is accurate at the time of going to press. The publisher welcomes information and suggestions for correction or improvement.